# The Journey That Matters: Lessons and Stories for Caregivers

Jodie Lightener

Copyright © 2012 Ralston Store Publishing

All rights reserved.

Ralston Store Publishing
P.O. Box 1684
Prescott, AZ 86302

ISBN 978-1-938322-04-4

Printed in the USA

This book is the simple story of a mother and a daughter struggling to make sense of life while time slips rapidly away.

* * * * *

If your parent is in a nursing home and you don't think the term "caregiver" applies to you, think again. Although someone else is taking care of your parent's day to day bodily needs, there is still plenty you can do—that you must do—to keep your parent healthy and happy.

# Table of Contents

I divided this book into meaningful chapters to give it some semblance of form. To look up nursing home specific topics, check the nursing home chapter. For health problems, check the health chapter. But just as you can't always place your life into neat little compartments, a parent's life can't always be evenly divided either. I tried to separate the information into logical categories to make it easier for the reader to get the exact information that he or she may be looking for.

| | |
|---|---|
| Introduction | 1 |
| 1. Beginnings: Are you Experienced? | 7 |
| 2. Transitions: From Innocent to Initiated | 26 |
| 3. Support: The Good, the Bad, and the Indifferent | 46 |
| 4. Emotions and Revelations: The Guilt Will Eat You Alive | 71 |
| 5. Dementia: Beam Me Up, Scotty! | 101 |
| 6. Health Issues: Sticks and Stones Can Break My Bones | 123 |
| 7. Sex, Drugs, and Rock 'n' Roll | 139 |
| 8. Nursing Home Issues: A Day in the Life | 148 |
| 9. The Home Alternative: Ain't No Place Like Home | 171 |
| 10. Gifts: Don't Look a Gift Horse in the Mouth | 183 |
| 11. Endgame: Aftermath | 198 |

# Introduction

<u>Living or Dying?</u>
Shortly after my mother's initial stroke and subsequent admission to the nursing home, there was a right to die initiative on our state ballot. Although I agree with the concept that humans should have the same freedom from pain and pursuance of dignity that animals are granted, I voted against it. I didn't want to be put in a position where I could decide whether my mother should live or die. Why do I begin a book with that thought? Because if your parent is incapacitated to the point of having flawed judgment, then you will be making that type of decision and more. If your parent's judgment is sound most of the time, you will still need the courage and strength to make sometimes difficult decisions.

<u>Because I'm the Mom</u>
You will not find many references to role reversal and parenting your parent in this book. I did use it a few times, but I tried to use the term

judiciously.  It is so easy to treat an invalid parent just like a child.  And a parent is not a child, and no matter how weak, irresponsible, and unable to take care of their own needs they may become, they still will not be children.  Treating a parent that way is demeaning to the parent.  One day my mother questioned me about paying one of her bills.  I responded that she would have to trust me.  Boy, was that the wrong thing to say!

When you tell a child no, "because I'm the mom" is a good enough reason.  That doesn't work with aging parents.  It doesn't matter what kind of physical or mental condition they are in—they are still your parents and you should treat them with respect.  A child has never made their own decisions, has never lived alone, has never paid bills or been responsible for money.  An aging parent has done all of those things.  They've been there and back.  Don't treat them as if they haven't, because it sets up a dynamic that is no good for either of you.  Do what you have to do to help your parents and keep them safe, but maintain respect while you do it.

A Wooden Bowl for You

How you handle your parental situation could come back to haunt you later.  If you have children, you are showing them how to treat you when your time comes.  There is a story that circulates on the Internet now and then that is based on an old folk tale.  An old man goes to live with his son, daughter-in-law, and their four-year-old son.  Because of the old man's poor eyesight and shaky hands, he often spills his drinks and occasionally breaks a dish.  The son decides that is not acceptable, and he seats the old man at a small table in the corner, with his food served in a wooden bowl. Some time after this, the parents come upon their four-year-old son fashioning something out of wood. When asked what he was doing, the boy said he was making a bowl for them to eat out of when they grow old. They changed their minds about the old man. The message is clear: treat your parents as you would like your children to treat you.

The choice to place your parents in a nursing home, to keep them in their own home, or to move them into your home remains one of the most difficult decisions ever faced. It is riddled with guilt, confusion, and anxiety. Mostly it remains a personal decision that people must come to in their own way and in their own time. Keep one important facet in mind while you decide your parent's future. Don't let a decision borne of guilt put your parent in an uncomfortable situation. If your parent is a gregarious person and craves socialization, think twice before you decide to leave them alone in your house with a nurse while you work all day. If it is available, adult day care may be preferable. The important thing to remember is that every situation is different and every person is different. Everyone must handle it in the way they can. There is no right or wrong.

<u>Finding the Balance</u>

One of the most difficult aspects of caregiving is finding balance. Many of us have families and a full time job in addition to the caregiving that we must do. It's almost like having three full time jobs. When it comes to squeezing everything in, many people often neglect themselves. I strongly urge you to move yourself up the priority list. If you get sick or if something happens to you, it won't do anyone any good. Take care of yourself first! Don't jeopardize your health or family to fulfill your caregiving obligations. Your parent would not want that to happen. My relationship with my mother improved when I stepped back, because I was less taxed and more relaxed. Find time for yourself and the dividends will surprise you.

<u>Mistakes and Forgiveness</u>
All parents make mistakes when raising their children, because their parents made mistakes when they were raised. The mistakes are passed from generation to generation. I mention some of my mother's mistakes in this book, but I meant her no harm by it. Forgiveness came long ago, before I even knew the extent of all her lessons. She gave me life, and more than that, she gave me the courage and tenacity to overcome adversity. How much is that worth? More than money can buy, I think.

<u>Gifts and Insights</u>
Many times in the two and a half years of my mother's tenure at the nursing home, I lamented over her circumstances. Not the nursing home itself—that wasn't part of the equation. The monumental factor was that she was still alive but she wasn't "whole." She never wanted that. She reminded me often over the years that it was my job to insure that never happened. I don't know what she expected me to do, but I obviously couldn't do it.

It wasn't until close to the end that I realized what a wonderful gift she had bestowed upon me. In those two and a half years I learned more about me, about her, and about our relationship, than in the previous fifty years. Although the challenges we faced were sometimes difficult for both of us to get through, in the end we were better off for it. She left behind a more peaceful familial world, and the insights that I gained will serve me well for the remainder of my life.

Most of those insights were realizations of the traits that I share with my mother. For some reason, the traits become magnified during these later years—especially the bad ones. And it is that magnification, I believe, that allows us to see which ones we share. In a way, it is like hearing your voice on a tape recorder for the first time. It feels familiar, but it's not immediately recognizable.

Helpers

The nurses, nurses' aides, nutritional aides, and helpers all deserve our deepest respect. These selfless individuals not only work long and hard hours for low wages, but they care about what they do and about the people they work with. Their job is one that I could never handle, and I have the greatest appreciation for them.

Sharing the Caregiving Experience

Something about the caregiving experience somehow encourages a person to share those experiences with others. Whether it is for information, commiseration, or validation, it feels like a strong need. For me, it was the many situations that caused me stress and frustration, and my desire to guide others along a path not so easy to navigate. "If I had only known!" became almost a mantra to me, with the insurance problems, nursing home complexities, and health issues. Hopefully, this book can help you help your aging parents on their journey that matters.

\* \* \* \* \*

Final note: I had told my mother that I was writing a book about our experiences together. One day she asked about the book. She said, "I don't know if you're going to include the bad things about me." I said, "Yes, I am." She said, "I think you should."

## Chapter 1
## Beginnings: Are You Experienced?

<u>The Unexpected</u>
    Where does one begin a story like this? Does it begin with a hunched-over little old woman struggling to get off a plane? (The same woman who just a year earlier was energetic and radiated vibrant health.) Or does it begin in the darkness at three in the morning when she called out that something was wrong, and my husband and I helped her into the bathroom where I watched my mom crinkle up and die? Her body survived the stroke that brought her there. But the mom I knew, the mom who had comforted and counseled and guided me through the years, was gone.
    The stroke affected her ability to walk, talk, and eat. Part of the time her speech was fine and unaffected. Sometimes she lapsed into "the mumbles," and you couldn't understand her at all. The nursing home kitchen solved her eating problems by either thickening her liquids or grinding up her solid foods. For her walking problems, she received physical therapy.
    My mom's condition devastated me. She couldn't walk, she couldn't use her left hand, and she had increasing difficulty talking and

remembering anything. Many times over the years, she had insisted that I "give her a push" (toward death) if her health or mind ever radically deteriorated. I knew I never could, but her words rang in my ears while I remembered the intensity in her voice as she spoke them. What I never expected was the new "partial Mother" clinging to life so vehemently.

When my mother's condition stabilized, the hospital immediately transferred her to a nursing home/rehabilitation center. There was never any question of whether or not she would come to my house instead of the nursing home. She needed intensive nursing involvement and rehabilitation that I could not provide.

> *Instead of denying your parent's aging process, prepare yourself and your parent for the unavoidable changes that will come. Make yourself aware of increasing health problems or any small changes in your elderly parent.*

## Background

My mom never wanted to stay with us. She had seen her share of interfering in-laws unintentionally destroy their children's marriages. She loved my husband and didn't want to do anything to jeopardize our relationship. Even when she stayed with us after her move from Arizona, she was eager to get an apartment and be back on her own. My mom loved living alone and cherished her freedom and independence. Several heart attacks and congestive heart episodes led to her staying at our house the night of her stroke.

Each one caused more damage, but Mom, indomitable spirit that she was, kept springing back to life.

Earlier that same year, her doctor had Mom hospitalized for some problem bleeding. When your parent is in her nineties or even eighties, with each hospital stay you wonder if it will be her last time. The thought always remains scary.

My mom always looked ten to twenty years younger than she was. It was difficult to think of her as ninety when she looked seventy. She never feared dying. Her only fear was looking or acting old. She refused to consider elder housing because she didn't want to "hang around with all those old people." Once I asked her if she wanted to go someplace and play bingo. She responded, "As long as everybody there isn't old!"

While in the nursing home and after I let her apartment go, my mother wanted to come live with us. This was something my real mom would *never* have wanted. That was one of the ways I discovered that my real mom was gone, never to return.

*Especially after a serious health event, your parent's attitudes and beliefs may change. Even steadfast beliefs and desires held for decades could change.*

<u>Nursing Home Introduction</u>
Getting used to the nursing home atmosphere wasn't easy. Too many people there looked like they were waiting to die. I wondered if my mother was one of them. Part of the pain of seeing her was seeing everyone else. Experiencing a nursing home is a full sensory ordeal. There's usually some moaning or calling

out going on, the occasional fecal matter or dirty hamster cage smell mixes with the antiseptic smell, and the sights, at least at first, are always sad. During my first visit I saw a woman without a nose.

The first days at the nursing home were difficult and distressing for me. Because she seemed so close to death, I was afraid to leave my mother's side. I sat there with her hour after hour, listening to her almost coherent conversation turn into the mumbles. My heart broke to see her like that. Just when I felt I couldn't take it anymore, her face would express what her words could not: that she wanted me to stay. And I would stay.

It was like sitting with a sick child, and probably my first real initiation into being my parent's parent. I felt touches of it before when doctors discussed her condition with me seeking my opinion. This, however, was something new. She'd ask me questions that exhibited her confusion. Where am I? Why am I here? What's wrong with me? And she'd ask other questions that revealed her stroke-induced dementia. Is Papa gone? Where's Mama? How many of my sisters are alive? I answered the same questions over and over again, day after day, and saw my beloved mom reduced to a sad old woman with some of her memories and some of her features. An old woman who sometimes couldn't remember her own name.

*The nursing home, or home care, represents a radical change in lifestyle. Be gentle with your parent and yourself. You may have a long way to go.*

Support
Experiencing too many different emotions at once caused me confusion and anguish. I didn't know what to think, I didn't know what to feel, and I didn't even know what to hope for. The ambiguity of the situation left me feeling helpless. The old mom never wanted what was occurring, but the new mother was hanging on and fighting for her life. Though I'm not religious myself, I turned to a religious friend for direction.

She quoted from the Bible, "A time to be born and a time to die." She said she had prayed that if this was my mother's time then to take her gently; but if it was not, then to give me the strength that I needed to endure.

My husband gave me tremendous support, as did some of my family. My friends were also there for me. At times like this, though, sometimes it feels like there isn't enough support out there to hold you up.

*During this time of tough decisions, heartbreaking moments, and struggles for independence, you need support. If someone in the family can provide that support, take it. If not, seek out a friend to help you through this. The social worker at the nursing home can always be of assistance or can recommend a support group to help you. Don't go through this alone.*


Down Will Come Baby, Cradle and All
At first, my mother's weakness limited her activities. She lay in bed like a lump without any options. Unless the nurse call button was close to

her right hand, she couldn't use it. Sometimes she appeared weaker than other times and she could not sit up by herself at all. Therefore, it was with great surprise that I received a phone call at seven in the morning that my mother had tried to get up in the middle of the night and had fallen out of bed. I spoke to her later that morning. She cried and said that she ached all over. I felt so bad, not only that she hurt, but she didn't yet understand the new limitations of her body.

That early morning phone call was the first of several calls about my mother's attempts to get out of bed by herself. After her first try, the nurses put a device on her that emitted a shrill noise if she moved too far. My mother, undaunted, figured a way around it and kept falling to the floor. Finally, they moved her bed to the ground. I had requested bars on the bed, but that wasn't possible. The social worker said there couldn't be any hint of restraint, either physical or chemical. (That's not true at all nursing homes.) She also said that if my mother were intent on getting out of bed, the bars would just make it a higher fall. That made sense, as I knew how determined my mother could be.

Even with her bed on the floor, she continually tried to climb out of it by herself. Luckily, there was nowhere to fall. She was already on ground level. After awhile, when her reality started to merge with everyone else's, she understood that she was too weak to get out of bed by herself.

While all this was going on and we were searching for a solution, one of my brothers kept pushing to have her sedated. Besides the nursing home not allowing it, I didn't feel it was right. Although my mother's quality of life had slipped to almost nothing, there were still people she enjoyed talking to and activities that she enjoyed. The sedatives would have limited her life even more than it was already limited.

*You may observe irrational behavior. Just as children become more responsible as they grow up, aging parents go in the opposite direction. It is up to you to make sure questionable situations are taken care of properly and promptly.*

## Fifth Demention
After my mother's initial confusion faded away, she announced that she had been "out of her mind," but now she was coming back. Unfortunately, that was only partially true. While she understood why she was there and what happened to her, she still sometimes had trouble with where she was. Several times I called her and she would tell me that she was in Iowa or Phoenix or Omaha. Then she would go on and on about how everything still looked the same and all the people were the same, but it's Iowa. Usually, I didn't see any justification or profit in telling her otherwise.

Her other main point of confusion concerned her parents. She'd often ask me about her mother or father. When I gently explained to her that they had already died, she wanted to know if I had attended their funeral. She didn't seem sad about it. She just blindly accepted the truth. The questions about her parents continued for awhile.

Another time I came to see her and she complained about the crowded conditions. I didn't understand. Just she and one other person shared a large room with plenty of space. My mother said she wanted to complain to management because a single bed was too small for two people. When I questioned her further, she told me that her sister, Bertha, shared the bed with her each night. Bertha had passed on almost twenty years earlier.

My mom always had a great imagination and it showed. One day she told me that they hadn't fed her the day before and they wouldn't let her out of bed. The day before I had spent several hours with her, watched them feed her, and knew she had spent a long time wheeling around. After a nap, she often forgot that she had already eaten. I told her to ask her roommate. When she asked her roommate, she would find that she had eaten a big meal before her nap.

One evening she called me and sounded upset. She kept saying the nurses wouldn't let her go home. She said she was in a different building, and they wouldn't let her go back to her original room. They were keeping her prisoner, and she wanted me to call the police. I spoke to a nurse, and she said my mother started in like that sometime around dinner. By the next day, she had forgotten all about the different building.

One day when I visited, she asked if she was still in high school. When I told her no, she informed me that she had to get a job. Sometime later she told my husband, Dan, that she wanted to go to college to become a teacher, so she could get a good pension. She had it all planned and wanted to take her classes in the morning, because she had things to do in the afternoon.

The severe dementia my mother suffered directly after her stroke was short-lived. Except for some mild and occasional relapses, her cognition returned to near normal and stayed that way most of the time.

*Be gentle and understanding with any type of dementia. Enjoy the stories, and get another view of what's inside your parent's mind. Your parent can't help what's going on, so don't blame them.*

The Apartment
The decision to give up my mother's apartment created much turmoil in my life. It took a long time after I made the decision to be at peace with it. What right did I have letting her apartment go? I still wasn't comfortable with the role reversal yet or even with my ability to make a decision like that.

My mother constantly talked about going home, and from her perspective her inability to walk was all that held her back. The physical therapist was amazed at her progress and thought she might recover completely. With all the mixed signals and the extreme consequences, I found it difficult to decide. My mother's love of her apartment and her longing to be back there hung over me like a cloud.

The need to make a quick decision about the apartment haunted me. Someone was interested in renting her apartment, and since my mom had signed a lease I thought that might be a good option. Because there was a time limit involved, I felt rushed.

After much difficulty, I finally decided to give up her apartment, but not tell her. I thought having her apartment to reach for was good incentive and important to her recovery. I feared that without that incentive, she would lose her motivation to walk. Keeping the information from her was another chore as there were other people involved—friends and neighbors from her apartment that sometimes came to visit. Luckily, everyone cooperated, and I could tell her gently in my own way.

Knowing my mother, I knew it would not work to tell her outright that I had already given up the apartment she loved. Instead, when she spoke of returning to it, I slowly began to suggest that with her current limitations her apartment might not be safe for her. There were other apartments better suited to her new needs. She didn't agree easily, but finally admitted that it might take longer to recover than she expected. It turned out that one of her main reasons for not wanting to give up the apartment was that she didn't want to hurt her landlord's feelings!

The decision to give up the apartment, although it felt difficult to make, should have been obvious. Her food still needed grinding, and she couldn't swallow liquids that weren't thickened. She still couldn't stand up by herself, and although her physical therapy progress reports showed a vast improvement, they hadn't seen her before the stroke. Even then she could barely walk by herself without wobbling. It all added up to not going back to that apartment. Unfortunately, I was too vulnerable and perhaps too close to the situation to see it clearly.

Besides the health difficulties that would have prevented her return to her apartment, there were other considerations as well. More than anything else my mother loved to read. After her stroke, she couldn't read at all. Her eyes weren't even good enough to watch television. She enjoyed participating in all the activities at the nursing home, and thrived on the social interaction. Mentally, her cognition had not returned to the point where she could take responsibility for herself. Until something changed, my mother needed to stay where she was.

Making the decision and telling my mother were only the first parts of the equation. The last part was the packing of the apartment. It affected me much more than I thought it would. Going through her belongings and deciding what would go into storage and what she might need in her present condition was emotionally exhausting and painful. I left her apartment each day feeling as if I had been hit in the stomach. It was a physical sensation.

Just packing boxes in her apartment, alone, without her there, was a reminder of what I had already lost. My mother was still alive, but the mom I knew, the mom I had grown up with and come to depend on, was gone. I think the act of deciding which belongings went where had more of an impact on me than seeing her have the stroke, hearing her struggle with words, or watching her lie helpless in her hospital bed. The whole incident may have been worse had she already died, but not filled with as much self-doubt or discomfort in my new role as her parent.

The trauma didn't end with packing up the apartment. Seeing the movers carting out her stuff and watching them put some of it in my house, was devastating. The implications of it felt greater than the event itself.

Even after I had cleaned the apartment and turned in the key, the residual effects of the stress lingered. Some relief had set in, but the anticlimactic feelings took their toll also. All this went on while my mother lay in her bed struggling to talk, struggling to walk, and yet still proclaiming and demanding her independence.

>  *Don't allow anyone to rush you through important decisions. Many decisions will become obvious if you are patient.*

Mix-up

Even after my mother knew that I'd given up her apartment, she'd still talk in vague terms about going home. She told me that her physical therapist had told her that she would be ready to go home soon. For a ninety-two year old woman, she had exceeded all expectations and surprised everyone with her rapid recovery. My mother gave me the impression that everybody thought she was almost ready to go home.

When the social worker asked me if I planned to take my mother home, I misinterpreted the question. I thought she was asking because she thought I should. After everything my mother had been telling me, I thought this was just another part of it.

For days I wrestled with my thoughts and my apprehensions about taking her home or getting her another apartment. I felt pressured by so-called authority figures from the nursing home—authority figures who were experienced in these matters. It wasn't right that they should encourage her and let her think that she was ready to go home. I felt that she was far from that option, and that in her clearer moments even she knew that. For the same reasons I had for giving up her apartment, I didn't feel it was time for her to go home yet. She still had the same limitations.

The situation angered me. The next time my mother mentioned them saying she was ready to go home, I bluntly told her that she couldn't even wipe her own butt. She reported to me the following day that when she had told them what I had said, they replied that I could wipe it for her!

Feeling frustrated, I decided to call the social worker to find out why we were so far apart regarding my mother's immediate future. When she heard who it was, she said she had been meaning to call me. She told me that my mother had said that I was planning to take her home, and that they didn't think she was ready. My mother was still getting physical therapy once or twice a day, and now was not the time to interrupt that. I laughed and told her that was exactly why I had called. Apparently, my mother had told each of us that the other said she should go home!

Like a little kid playing one parent against the other, my mother had manipulated both of us into believing something that wasn't true. She wasn't exactly lying—she was telling the truth as she knew it. When her physical therapist told her she was doing a great job, she interpreted that to mean she could go home. My mother practiced selective listening: she heard what she wanted to hear.

Once I found out the truth, it was easier to handle my mother's comments. I knew why she did it. She was reaching out for the independence she either knew or suspected was gone forever.

*Follow up on any statement from your parent that doesn't sound right. Ask questions to verify. It's not that a person after a lifetime of telling the truth suddenly turns to lies. It's just that their reality isn't always consistent with ours.*

## Family Ties

When your parent has a debilitating stroke, especially after a series of heart attacks, it shocks you from your normal complacency. The person you once considered invincible is now lying helpless in a bed. For my family, this event began a process of healing that we all needed.

My oldest brother wrote to tell me that he had an "awakening" and thought that he needed to come to Massachusetts. He and my mother, once very close, in recent years had irreconcilable differences and only spoke occasionally. Their strained relationship combined with her current condition made him uncomfortable. Although it was too late to discuss the trouble that had come between them, it was not too late to pay his respects and tell her that he loved her. He took the next flight out, hoping to heal the wound that had festered for far too long.

A cousin suggested that I try to persuade my Aunt Connie to come see my mother. She and my mother had been extremely close for about seventy years, but shortly after my mother's first heart attack they had a falling-out. I somehow got involved in the events and misunderstandings leading to the disagreement. That caused a rift between Connie and me and deepened the rift between her and my mother. Mom didn't even say good-by to Connie when she moved from Phoenix to Massachusetts. The situation was heartbreaking and unfortunate for two sisters in their older years.

Several months before her stroke, Mom had watched an Oprah segment on the book, *Tuesdays with Morrie*, by Mitch Albom. It touched her and made her cry. She immediately asked me to buy the book and send it to Connie. Since then, they spoke periodically and had an uneasy truce.

When Connie found out about the stroke, she immediately called me to find out how Mom was and told me she planned to leave right away. She rode in the ambulance with Mom when they transferred her from the hospital to the nursing home. I think her presence made the transition easier. Again too late to discuss or repair old injuries, it was not too late to affirm the love between them.

*In a crisis situation, contact everyone associated with your parent. Give them the opportunity to heal old wounds or make their peace.*

Visiting Hours
    Whenever my mom was in the hospital, I visited her every day. Shortly after her first stroke, there was an event planned weeks earlier that I couldn't reschedule. I had to attend. I started telling my mother a couple days before that I couldn't be there Sunday. She said she would miss me, but she was okay with it.

When I came to see her Monday, she went on and on how much she missed me. She made me feel very guilty about skipping a day. The doctor came in shortly after. He asked how she was, and she said that she was feeling better today, but yesterday she wasn't doing too well since she was alone all day.

The doctor left shortly after that, and I followed him outside to see what he thought about her condition. He said that she had been quite manipulative with those comments. His comment shocked and enlightened me. I knew she made me feel guilty and I knew she did it often. However, I didn't realize it was manipulation. Once I became aware of this, I could avoid some of the guilty feelings.

Later, after she was in the nursing home, I began to cut my visits down and didn't go every day. I would still make sure we talked every day. That wasn't enough for my mother. When I'd call, she would start right in about how good it felt when she saw me and how lonely she always was. I explained that I couldn't visit every day, but she never accepted that. She always wanted more from me than I could give. Even when I did come to see her, she'd ask if I was coming the following day. When I would say no, she would then tell me how important my visits were to her. She knew how to make me feel guilty.

My niece called my mother while I was away on a brief business trip. My mother thought it was me and started in on her about how bad she felt, and how I should come to see her more often. When my mother realized it wasn't me, she immediately lightened up and told my niece she was feeling fine and doing well. My niece said even her tone of voice changed.

Once I went to see her after not visiting for a couple days. She was lying in bed looking especially weak. She cried when I came in. I asked her what was wrong, and she said she thought she was dying. Later in the conversation she kissed my hand and told me that was the last kiss. Before I left, she told me to tell my husband, Dan, good-by. I left there in tears. The next day when I went in, she was feeling great and had forgotten all about what she had said the day before. We'll never know if she was really feeling that way and thinking those thoughts, or if she just said that to punish me for not visiting.

My mother had another manipulation that she started in the beginning and used periodically. I would close every conversation with, "I love you." Sometimes she would say, "I don't think you do." When I asked her why she would say that, she never gave me a straight answer. It was always over some real or imagined slight that I had no idea about.

The real clincher came one evening as I wheeled my mother's wheelchair into the dining room, so she could have dinner with the other residents. In a loud and clear voice she announced to everyone in the room, "This is my daughter. She only comes to visit me once or twice a week." A nurse helping with dinner told her that was more than most people had visitors. I left there embarrassed and furious. When I told a friend about the incident, she said it sounded like a mother-daughter sitcom! That made me laugh and I'm laughing now as I write this, but at the time I felt really angry.

*All of us, with different lives and different responsibilities, can only give what we can. Don't feel guilty over your limitations.*

\* \* \* \* \*

Points to Remember:

1. Instead of denying your parent's aging process, prepare yourself and your parent for the unavoidable changes that will come. Make

yourself aware of increasing health problems or any small changes in your elderly parent.

2. Especially after a serious health event, your parent's attitudes and beliefs may change. Even steadfast beliefs and desires held for decades could change.

3. The nursing home, or home care, represents a radical change in lifestyle. Be gentle with your parent and yourself. You may have a long way to go.

4. During this time of tough decisions, heartbreaking moments, and struggles for independence, you need support. If someone in the family can provide that support, take it. If not, seek out a friend to help you through this. The social worker at the nursing home can always be of assistance or can recommend a support group to help you. Don't go through this alone.

5. You may observe irrational behavior. Just as children become more responsible as they grow up, aging parents go in the opposite direction. It is up to you to make sure questionable situations are taken care of properly and promptly.

6. Be gentle and understanding with any type of dementia. Enjoy the stories, and get another view of what's inside your parent's mind. Your parent can't help what's going on, so don't blame them.

7. Don't allow anyone to rush you through important decisions. Many decisions will become obvious if you are patient.

8. Follow up on any statement from your parent that doesn't sound right. Ask questions to verify. It's not that a person after a lifetime of telling the truth suddenly turns to lies. It's just that their reality isn't always consistent with ours.

9. In a crisis situation, contact everyone associated with your parent. Give them the opportunity to heal old wounds or make their peace.

10. All of us, with different lives and different responsibilities, can only give what we can. Don't feel guilty over your limitations.

### Excerpt from My Journal:

*Having to see your parent like this is so cruel. It really is something that nobody should have to go through. But in a way, isn't it the natural ending to the circle of life? Your parent watches you grow from infant to toddler to child and beyond. And then at the end, you watch your parent go from adult to elder to aged and then gone. The completion of a circle. But when you watch a child grow, there is hope and promise in their smile. As you watch your parent grow closer to death, it's hard to see anything but sadness in their smile.*

# Chapter 2
## Transitions: From Innocent to Initiated

### Incorrect Assumption

The night my mom had her stroke, I thought I was watching her die. She had been staying at our house because of her recent heart attack. About three o'clock in the morning, she called to me that her left hand was shaking and she needed help getting to the bathroom. She said she had felt weird since about midnight, but didn't want to wake me up. I went downstairs to help her, and she struggled to stand up. I called to my husband, and he hurried downstairs. With my mother supported between us, we held her up as she shuffled one step at a time toward the bathroom.

Once in the bathroom, I helped pull down her pants, and she sat on the toilet. With her face crinkled up, she leaned to one side with her eyes tightly shut. Her speech faded to gibberish. My husband called the ambulance while I stayed with my mother, trying to comfort her and making sure she didn't fall.

Until the ambulance came, she remained leaning against the wall. The paramedics carefully eased her off the toilet and onto the stretcher. I thought she was a goner. At that moment, I knew I had just watched my mother die, and it was just a matter of time before she drew her last breath. It was a terrible time. They wouldn't let me stay in the back of the ambulance with her, so I sat in the front seat. Fifteen minutes later when we were almost to the hospital, I heard my mother in the back of the ambulance! She was talking again! By the time she entered the emergency room, she had almost completely recovered.

After some tests, they admitted her to the hospital. She had problems with her left side and couldn't use her left leg or her left hand. Most of the time her speech was normal, although it sometimes deteriorated into the mumbles. She tried to express her thoughts, but they just wouldn't come out.

The second day she was in the hospital another stroke gripped her, crinkling her face and taking away her speech once more. Again I thought I was watching her last breaths on earth. And again she defied death and came back fighting. This second stroke affected her right hand, but she recovered complete use again by the end of the day. My mom was tough.

*The fear of losing a parent can be as painful as the loss itself. Whether or not the death occurs at that time does not mean the fear of loss hurts any less.*

## Getting Used to Tough Changes

My mom wasn't in the hospital very long before they transferred her to the nursing home. For several days she just lay there, unable to do anything by herself. I didn't dare pray or even wish for her survival, because I didn't think that's what she wanted. She lay there helpless and distressed, and I didn't want to prolong her suffering.

The enormity of the changes within her hit me when she recovered enough to move around on her own. I had always confided in my mom about almost everything in my life. While I didn't always follow her advice, I always requested it. Suddenly, I couldn't do that anymore. Now, the person whose advice I once sought couldn't even make her own decisions.

The loss of my mom as a confidant and trusted friend hit me especially hard. My mother was still there, but the mom I knew and relied on was gone forever. Having to make decisions for her, and about her, only served to reinforce my loss. Her presence there and yet not there, was particularly painful for me.

*The loss of a parent doesn't have to mean losing them to death. I felt the loss of my mom very deeply, although she was still alive. Getting used to the "new mother" was twice as hard, because I was still grieving for the loss of my "original mom."*

## Getting Used to More Changes

It was my Aunt Connie who straightened me out. When we spoke on the phone, I told her of some strange behavior and offbeat conversations I had with my mother. She said, "Don't you realize she has brain damage?" Astounded, I was silent. She said, "Didn't you know that?" There had been talk of damaged pathways, and I knew my mother wasn't right. However, no one before had ever said those two words together: brain damage. It seemed obvious, but this simple truth had eluded me. This new knowledge explained a lot!

Aunt Connie also said that my mother told her how much she liked it in the nursing home and what a good time she had there. Aunt Connie said, "You know your mother would never have wanted to live like this. That alone shows how far she's slipped."

What I learned from that conversation was that the wants and needs of the "new mother" were not always what the "original mom" would have wanted. It was now up to me to decide what was best for her. She could not do that for herself. I didn't like making decisions that affected another human being's future. It was especially difficult because I hadn't expected such serious responsibility.

*While heart attacks damage the heart and cause heart damage, strokes damage the brain and cause brain damage. How large the stroke is and its location determine the seriousness of the damage. Multiple strokes often mean new and different changes for you and your parent to adjust to.*

## The First Thanksgiving

My mother had been in the nursing home for a couple months when Thanksgiving came around. Although I visited regularly, I didn't know too much about her abilities or her limitations. The first Thanksgiving I shared with her at the nursing home woke me up to both.

For the previous twenty years or so, my mother had coughing spells. Just after we sat at the table she began one of them. But her mouth was different this time and she couldn't control it. Like a baby learning to eat solid food, her mouth was out of her control.

When the food came, I saw a silver metal attachment that fit on the edge of the plate to keep food from falling off. My mother still struggled to get it on her fork. The silverware had thick rubber over the handles to make them easier to hold. She held them like a child might. Even with that, she barely managed to keep them in her hands. She ate like someone just learning to use utensils, and indeed she was. It was especially tragic because my mom used to love working with her hands, and she was very adept at it. Seeing her like this, barely able to manage, saddened me.

The kitchen staff had ground up her food and thickened the liquid in her glass. The food needed grinding because after her stroke she had trouble swallowing. And her liquid needed thickening for the same reason.

That Thanksgiving was an illuminating and disheartening experience. It was so sad seeing her like that. It was so sad seeing exactly how far my mom had slipped. But this was not my mom. This person needed looking after just like a child.

What got to me was that she still spoke of returning to her apartment. This woman had a hard time functioning with twenty-four hour help! Her unproven confidence in herself did resonate with the virtues of the old mom, though. She always believed she could do anything she wanted.

*After a stroke, heart attack, or other debilitating illness, always try to see your parent "in action" before making any judgments or decisions affecting their welfare. Routine visits where you see them stand up and sit down often won't give you enough information.*

## Out With the Old, In with the New, Again

After several months passed, my mother and I settled into a new relationship. It may have been the same as before, but it felt different because I was dealing with the "new mother." I'd wheel her around and we'd sit and talk, and everything had started feeling almost comfortable. Then the unexpected happened. She changed. Again.

One morning I received a call from the head nurse. She said that the night before, my mother had become agitated and had "beaten up" one of the nurses! My mother had pushed, punched, kicked, and spit and wouldn't let anyone near her. Because she refused to take a sedative by mouth, they had to give her a shot to settle her down.

The following day wasn't my normal day for visiting, but my mother's activities the night before concerned me. I walked up and found her sitting in front of the nurses' station. When she saw me she started laughing hysterically.

We went into the day room and had a conversation that made little sense to me. She kept asking confusing questions about money. I told her that I didn't understand what she was asking. Suddenly she looked at me angrily and said, "I can't trust you! I found out you're no good!" Stunned, I just stared at her. Then she blurted out, "Wipe that smile off your crooked face!" I'd had enough and I left. Regardless of her mental state, having your mother tell you to your face that you're no good, still hits harder than you can imagine.

The consensus was that she had another stroke or was about to have another stroke. The physical therapist mentioned that she was not doing well, especially with her left hand. All of this left me shattered. I was just getting used to the "new mother" and now she was gone and an even "newer mother" had taken her place. I didn't think I liked the latest one. My husband, Dan, said that maybe she would get back to where she had been, but I wasn't sure. It all depended on which pathways this latest stroke damaged and how damaged they were.

Saturday when I went to visit, her first question was about her checkbook, and I thought the whole ugly scene was starting again. When I called her on Sunday, again that was her first question. She couldn't see and she couldn't write. She had no concept of her bills or her income. There was no way I could give her access to her checkbook in her present condition. Nor could I tell her that. What was it about a ninety-three year old woman who couldn't walk, but who could blow my emotions around like they were bubbles in the wind? It was only because she was my mother and had a long history of pushing my buttons.

During my mother's thirty months at the nursing home, she had several more strokes and went through many more changes. Just when I got comfortable with the situation, it would change. It was a constant struggle to adapt. My mother was going through many changes and she didn't even realize it.

*Once your parent's health begins to decline, it's likely there will be many more changes to come. Be prepared for them, and try to handle them with gentleness and grace.*

## Mirror, Mirror on the Wall

Vanity always defined my mom. What she always strived for was looking good and having people tell her that she looked good. After her stroke she retained some of that, especially making sure that her clothes always matched and looked nice. However, the most defining aspect of her vanity disappeared. That was her wig.

She bought the wig many years before and only told two people: me and her sister Connie. If anyone else mentioned that her hair looked different, she told them that she had gone to a different beauty salon. As years passed, she confided in a few more people, but not many. She always claimed that her hair started falling out after her brain surgery, but I suspect it was more medication-related. Regardless, she had very little hair at the time of her stroke.

Her wig and keeping the secret of her wig were of utmost importance to my mom. Several months before her stroke, my brother came from overseas to visit her. The two of them had just arrived at my house, and my brother was upstairs looking around. Our four-month old puppy, who my mom had seen many times before, had developed a new habit of jumping. When she saw my mom, she jumped up in glee. My mom, unsteady on her feet anyway, toppled over. For me it was like watching something in slow motion. The puppy was between my mom and me. There was nothing I could do. As my mom tilted back, I saw her wig fly off her head. Even if she had broken her hip with the bone poking through the skin, I knew her first thought would not be the pain, but the wig. As if on cue, when she hit the ground she reached for it just as I picked it up to hand it back to her.

Luckily no broken bones occurred, but it was an enlightening experience. The only ones in the house were my brother, my husband, and me. Three people who already knew about the wig.

During her first days at the nursing home, she wore a little night hat that I had brought her. She didn't care if it was on or not. If it fell off at night or in the daytime, she showed no inclination to put it back on. People came in and out of the room, and she didn't even try to hide her almost bald head. Even many months later after she recovered most of her sensibilities, she still showed no sensitivity for anyone seeing her without her wig.

While living at the nursing home, my mother had to visit the hospital emergency room several times. Usually they didn't send along her night hat or her wig. Knowing how the old mom would have reacted to that, I always made an effort to bring back the night hat on my next visit. One time in the emergency room, she again arrived with a bare head. Doctors, nurses, and technicians entered and exited the room and she showed no sensitivity to their presence. I asked her why it didn't bother her for strangers to see her bald head. She said that things change. She said that she didn't used to tell people her age, but at ninety she decided to start telling. Now, her bald head didn't bother her anymore, either. The explanation felt too simple.

Experiencing her lack of reaction firsthand brought home to me the dramatic difference between the new mother and my original mom.

Knowing the enormity of the secret and how important the wig was to her, I never expected or got used to her new flippant attitude toward her wig.

> *Personality changes may occur after a stroke or other serious illness. Even core personality traits may disappear completely or transform into something entirely different. Although your parent's essence remains, some of the intrinsic qualities that define that essence may be gone or changed forever. It's difficult to get used to.*

## Love Is Just a Four Letter Word

When my mom was in the hospital and during her initial time in the nursing home, she would delight in my presence. She received pleasure just from seeing me, just from having me around. She would gaze into my eyes almost like a lover. I would hold her hand or stroke her arm and try to give her strength. This served me well until she overcame her weakness and started resuming a somewhat normal, if different, life in the nursing home.

My first indication of a change happened early in her stay when we were on the phone. She told me that she missed me and wanted to see me. Why? Because she wanted me to bring her something.

The second indication came less than two weeks later. When I arrived to visit, she was in someone else's room. After I found her, we went out into the hall to talk, where she began to complain about something. When she finished complaining, she immediately began to return to her friend Lucille's room. Hoping that she was establishing friendships there, I asked her if she liked Lucille. She said, "No, I just didn't have anything else to do." We talked a few more minutes when she again started going into Lucille's room. I said, "Why don't we stay out here for a while, because we can't talk in there." She said, "Then you can sit and listen to us," and she turned her wheelchair and proceeded into the room.

Following her into the room, I sat there and listened to them talk. Suddenly Lucille made a comment that I knew would irritate my mother. "Don't you want to leave now?" my mother asked me. I thought she was using that so we could go outside and continue talking. Instead, when I got up to leave, it became obvious that she was going to stay!

From this encounter I learned two lessons. The first was that since actions speak louder than words, although she said she didn't like Lucille, it was obvious that she did. The second was that she preferred spending time with Lucille rather than quality time with me. It made me feel both bad and good. Bad, because of the rejection. Good, because it meant that she had begun to make a new life for herself.

The situation again demonstrated how my role in my mother's life had changed. In her remaining time at the nursing home, I gradually evolved into the role of a servant. When I came to visit, she always had a job waiting for me. Whether it was putting away clothes, plucking her eyebrows, or clipping her toenails, there was always something to do. It was almost like she had a list. She didn't long to hear the sound of my voice. She didn't yearn to see me. I was just another servant to her. The days of her delighting in my presence were only a memory.

> As your parent changes with time, your role in your parent's life may also change. Recognize the change, and as much as it might hurt, go with the flow.

## Picture Perfect

There was a bulletin board next to each bed. Pinned to my mother's were pictures of her great grandchildren, me and my husband, my brother and his wife, and our dog. When her roommate moved out to go into a different section of the nursing home, my mother transferred her belongings to the window side of the room. The pictures never made it over there. Shortly after, my mother also moved to the other section of the nursing home. There she sat with another empty bulletin board.

I felt devastated and angry. Her pictures! I was ready to go to the administrator of the nursing home and demand to get back her pictures. They were so important—to me. It took me awhile to come to this truth. Although I was broken up over the loss of the pictures, my mother didn't even know they were gone. I don't even think she could see them. The pictures gave me comfort while I was there visiting, and I think that's why it upset me. But they didn't do anything for her. Never one for sentimentality anyway, my mother didn't care about the pictures. She enjoyed seeing them when I first brought them. But once they went up on the bulletin board, just far enough away to be unrecognizable by her failing eyes, they might as well have been placed in the trash. They weren't her concern.

Before protecting or defending your parent, make sure they require it. Sometimes what you perceive as their issue is really yours.

## Riding Shotgun

My mother wanted me to take her for a ride in the car. She said she hadn't been out in months. I didn't want to take her, and I felt terribly guilty about it. My mother was continent, but sometimes she just barely made it to the bathroom. Sometimes, it was a minute too late. I didn't want to have to deal with that. After a torturous, gut-wrenching debate with myself, guilt won, and I was prepared to tell her that I would take her.

Having overcome what I thought were selfish reasons for not wanting to go, I felt good about myself when I walked in that day. Fifteen minutes later, I was furious. My mother and I were about to leave the room, and she wanted her roommate to do something for her. Instead of asking politely, with a "please" and a "thank-you," she demanded it in an aggressive, abusive voice. As soon as we got away from the area, I told her that she had to stop acting like that. I told her that if she ever did it again in front of me that I would leave immediately. I'd seen her treat people poorly before, but this was the worst.

That was the end of the ride business. Months later when she started asking again, I decided the best way to handle it would be to hire someone else to take her for rides. It made perfect sense to me. She would get her ride, she would have someone else to talk to, and I wouldn't have to do it. For a difficult situation, I thought it was the perfect solution. But I felt uncomfortable handling it like that. What if someone asked why I couldn't do it myself? How would I answer? Those thoughts made me feel ashamed of myself. So, in a moment of weakness, I relented.

After putting plastic on the seat of the car, I helped her in. She didn't appear that excited about getting out in the world again. We rode around for a while, and I took her to some of my favorite places, but she acted uninterested. Not long after we started, she said she was ready to go back home. She said her back hurt. Why it would hurt in the car and not in her wheelchair, I didn't know. I thought maybe it was just an excuse to get back to more familiar surroundings. She never asked about a ride again.

*Sometimes what you resist isn't as bad as it seems. Giving in to something that you don't want to do is often easier than listening to constant requests. An alternative is hiring someone else.*

### Which Came First, the Chicken or the Egg?

Following an unusually disruptive occurrence, my mother's doctor felt it necessary to have her mental health checked by a geriatric consultation team. He wanted to find out whether all of her mini-strokes had caused her behavior or if something else caused it.

I didn't know exactly when the team was coming. One day when I came to see her, I was surprised to find her in an office talking to them. When they finished most of her evaluation, they invited me in to answer a few questions. Entering the room, I found my mother beaming with happiness. She was thrilled with the attention and the challenge of it all.

The incident made me feel gladdened and saddened. Seeing her that ecstatic with the attention made me happy. I couldn't get over how she sparkled, and how much fun she had. What upset me was the tiresome routine that our visits had become. It made me wonder where I had gone wrong.

Why were our visits together so miserable? After taking care of the little jobs she saved for me, I would spend the rest of our time together watching the clock for when I could go home. It felt like her conversation always revolved around complaints or insults toward me or those around her. Because I hated listening to that, I dreaded our visits.

Which came first, my wanting to leave, or her complaints and negativity? Thinking it was me, I felt guilty and decided to start fresh. Although I didn't have much confidence that I could turn the situation around, I vowed to myself that I would try. I wanted it to work so I wouldn't dread my visits anymore. I wanted it to work so I could give my mother more enjoyment in her life.

The next day on the phone, I told her that I was bringing over a deck of cards so we could play. She said, "You don't spend enough time here to play cards." Undaunted, I said, "Maybe I would if we could do something that was fun." Her reply was that she thought putting away her clothes was fun. She was just being contrary, and I refused to let her get to me.

That afternoon I brought the cards. It turned out to be a sobering experience. I went in with a joyous and hopeful attitude and came out feeling sad. Since that morning when I talked to her, she had had another mini-stroke.

When I came in she was sleeping, and I had a hard time waking her. Almost the whole time I was there, she slept. A few times she woke up and asked a weird question, like, "What side am I on, right or left?" Her mouth drooped open and she drooled down the front of her shirt. Her top teeth dropped to meet the lower, giving her face a grotesque appearance.

This affected me deeply. Here I was with a great attitude trying to take a new turn in our relationship, and it looked like she was on death's doorstep. I didn't want her to die before I had a chance to change what had become boring and painful for both of us. Luckily, she didn't.

A couple days later she was back to normal. Next time I came to visit, I brought the cards. After taking care of her clothes, we played a few hands and both enjoyed it.

My great attitude didn't last long, however. We played cards a few times, and she was fine. Then, one day in the activity room between games, we were having a pleasant conversation. Suddenly she said, "See that woman sitting across from you? Do you see how fat she is?" The woman was fewer than ten feet away and could have heard the comment. I pleaded with her to stop. A few minutes later, another woman parked her wheelchair just outside the door. My mother said, "See all those black marks on her arms?" She just couldn't quit with the insults. That's when I knew that her negativity had come first, and my watching the clock was just a byproduct of her disparaging comments.

You can't always control what your visits with your parent become. Sometimes you can make changes for the better. You owe it to yourself and your parent to try.

## Be Careful What You Wish For

During the first few weeks of my mother's stay at the nursing home, it was painful for me when she spoke of returning home. Initially, I had no idea if it was possible or not. Later when I realized that it was extremely unlikely, it tore me up even more. At first, I told her that she couldn't return home until she could walk again. That seemed reasonable, and my mother had every intention of walking out of there. For a while, it even looked like she might.

After her physical therapist told her she would never walk again unassisted, it still didn't quell her desire to have her own apartment. She still spoke of it often. Of course, it wasn't possible. She still needed her food ground up, she still couldn't drink liquids without thickening, and she was not aware enough to take her medications. Plus, if she fell down, which she still did occasionally, she couldn't get up again by herself.

I don't know what changed. It felt like she hadn't asked about going home for quite awhile. When I thought about it, I couldn't remember the last time she had mentioned it. This realization really affected me. It made me sad that she had deteriorated so much that she didn't find her living conditions offensive. Although anyone else would consider them more than adequate, they were living conditions that she never would have accepted while she was whole.

Your parent may make statements that bother you. But it might bother you more when they stop saying them.

\* \* \* \* \*

Points to Remember:

1. The fear of losing a parent can be as painful as the loss itself. Whether or not the death occurs at that time does not mean the fear of loss hurts any less.
2. Losing a parent can also be losing the "original parent" and getting used to the new parent they've become.
3. While heart attacks damage the heart and cause heart damage, strokes damage the brain and cause brain damage. How large the stroke is and its location determine the seriousness of the damage. Multiple strokes often mean new and different changes for you and your parent to adjust to.
4. After a stroke, heart attack, or other debilitating illness, always try to see your parent "in action" before making any judgments or decisions affecting their welfare. Routine visits where you see them stand up and sit down often won't give you enough information.
5. Once your parent's health begins to decline, it's likely there will be many more changes to come. Be prepared for them, and try to handle them with gentleness and grace.
6. Personality changes may occur after a stroke or other serious illness. Even core personality traits may disappear completely or transform into something entirely different. Although your parent's essence remains, some of

the intrinsic qualities that define that essence may be gone or changed forever. It's difficult to get used to.

7. As your parent changes with time, your role in your parent's life may also change. Recognize the change, and as much as it might hurt, go with the flow.

8. Before protecting or defending your parent, make sure they require it. Sometimes what you perceive as their issue is really yours.

9. Sometimes what you resist isn't as bad as it seems. Giving in to something that you don't want to do is often easier than listening to constant requests. An alternative is hiring someone else.

10. You can't always control what your visits with your parent become. Sometimes you can make changes for the better. You owe it to yourself and your parent to try.

11. Your parent may make statements that bother you. But it might bother you more when they stop saying them.


## Excerpt from an Email:

To my brother after he wrote saying we should take away her (prescription) medication:

The mom that we knew is gone. This one has some of the same memories, and the same words and the same looks, but she is only a shadow of what she once was. It's sad. It's very sad. It tears me up every day. I've lost my mom, and this new person that I have to deal with reminds me of it each and every day. But this new person wants to live, and who are we to decide otherwise? She loves her bingo. Is that enough? I don't know. She still gets joy out of life. Maybe *not as much joy as you and I would wish for our mother, but it seems to be enough for her. It's very sad. It's profoundly sad. But she has an incredible will to live . . .*

# Chapter 3
## Support: The Good, the Bad, and the Indifferent

Definition

What constitutes support? Money? Time? Love? Good intention? Support means different things to different people. I think it even means different things at different times. How much support is "enough" support? When I was going over the material for this book, I noticed that one person who I didn't think was very supportive, had been extremely supportive in the beginning —writing almost every day. It eventually dwindled down to once in a while. The beginning of the parental crisis is always more real to people on the outskirts. Once the newness wears off and it's down to the nitty-gritty of everyday living, many of your initial supporters will dwindle away. Can you blame them? I've often wondered if someone else had been handling this, how supportive would I have been? How much of myself would I give if I wasn't obligated by sheer proximity? I'd like to think that I would continue giving much of myself, as I was the only one to speak to my mother every week for as long as I can remember. But I don't think there's any way to really know.

Being in a situation where you are the sole caregiver of your aging parent sometimes feels like being dead. Everybody else's life goes on like nothing is different, but you are caught in a carousel of pain, drama, and emotion. Your reality doesn't change from day to day—your parent's issues and the inherent problems that go with those issues are always there. Everyone else's life moves onward but you're stuck in the wings while life continues to go by. When my mother was diagnosed with lung cancer, I received many condolences and "I'm sorrys" and words of comfort. But I was the only one who carried the emotional baggage which a diagnosis like that brings with it.

There are many types of support, and believe me, you will need them all when you're going through these trying times. Some people will call, write, and be there to hold your hand. Some will advise, counsel, and commiserate. Some people will visit your parent when you aren't able to. Some will send cards and letters and call your parent on the phone. Remember, any support given to your parent is indirectly given to you.

Sometimes support can be as simple as a surprise phone call from a stranger. One time my mother was nagging me to call the dentist, who I had called several times already. She asked for the number, so I just gave it to her, not thinking if she would be able to remember the number. I received a phone call a few minutes later from someone introducing herself as Mrs. So-and-so from a nearby town and asking if I was Iris's daughter. Then she explained that my mother had called her (her phone number was a digit or two off from the dentist) to ask a question. Mrs. So-and-so asked if my mother was at the nursing home and said she had one there, too. We only spoke for a few minutes, but for some reason when I got off the phone, I felt like I had been hugged. I think just having that small reminder that I wasn't the only one going through this comforted me. That simple phone call from a stranger meant more to me than the "good intentions" of many family members.

*There are many types of support, and during these trying times you will need them all. Sometimes, those who you expected to be most supportive won't be. And sometimes, someone you never expected to be supportive at all, will step forward to help. Never say no to any support that is offered.*

## Legal Support

When my mom moved here from Arizona, she felt she should update her will in conjunction with Massachusetts laws. Her lawyer, luckily, suggested giving me Power of Attorney in case anything happened. Ironically, she signed the papers in the hospital after her heart attack. By the time she was debilitated by the stroke, everything was already in place.

The importance of having someone designated as Power of Attorney is manyfold. As soon as my mother was admitted to the nursing home, I had to sign several documents. You do not want to take personal responsibility for your parent's debts at this time. If your parents have no money, there are programs in place to take care of them. If they do have money, as Power of Attorney, you are promising to pay their bills with their money. You should not have to pay a dollar of your own money for anything except personal or comfort items for your parent. This is the financial Power of Attorney.

The medical directive also comes into play at this time. The nursing home or the hospital will need to have a copy of it. Unless your parent happened to have it on them at the time of the circumstance that brought them there, you will be relied on to supply it. Just saying no to life support or yes to life support isn't enough. What if your parent is suffering? Should drugs be given to comfort them? All this needs to be written down beforehand. This is the medical Power of Attorney or Durable Power of Attorney.

Who should be designated the Power of Attorney? Someone emotionally and physically close to your parent should be the "POA." If you are the favored son or daughter, but you live three thousand miles away, forget about suggesting yourself. Find someone in the general proximity who is trustworthy and willing to accept the task. Who is trustworthy? That is a stickier question since many people who appear reliable have their own agenda. Someone who you may trust with your money, you may not trust with your children, and vice versa. Find someone you would (and your parent would) trust with their money and their life.

My mom used to have this story about her father telling her mother how to save money once he was gone. My grandmother used to say, "I don't have to worry. Steven will take care of me." Steven was her eldest son. As it turned out, by the time my grandmother needed taking care of, Steven was married and more interested in taking care of his mother-in-law than his own mother. Some trust is misplaced. Try to anticipate problems beforehand.

*Anyone can have a debilitating stroke or some other devastating thing happen. A Power of Attorney (both financial and medical) should be as mandatory as a will. If you will not be the designee, find someone trustworthy. Different states have different rules regarding these documents.*

## Pressure from Afar

Medicare paid for the first hundred days of my mother's care. The definition for "skilled nursing" is nebulous, but my mother qualified because she received physical therapy. When the one hundred days ended, or when the end was approaching, the pressure from family began.

The nursing home where my mother lived was expensive. In comparison with other nursing homes, it was about average. But if this was your first introduction, then the monthly expenditure seemed excessive. Certain members from my family pressured me to find something cheaper. My mother, despite her longing to go home, enjoyed the place tremendously. She participated in all the activities, knew almost everyone by name, and enjoyed the social outlets there.

My dilemma was in deciding to uproot her from a place she liked, just to save a few dollars. After some research, it turned out there weren't many choices. This is a fairly small town with limited facilities. There was either a place with inferior services or a place that was far away. Since I held the Power of Attorney for my mother, it was my responsibility to do what was best for her—not what was best for the family. If she lived far from me and I couldn't see her as often, that would hurt her and possibly affect her recovery. The other place wasn't even considered.

The decision upset people, but that didn't bother me. I felt I was doing the right thing. It wasn't our money that my mother was borrowing. It was her money until she died, and as long as I was in charge, that money would go to making her as comfortable and happy as she could possibly be in her present circumstances.

*If you have the Power of Attorney, or if you are responsible for making decisions like this, remember that your parent's well-being is the most important thing to consider. Ignore the pressure and do what's right, or as my mom used to say, "Follow your heart."*

Better Half

My mom's move to Massachusetts affected my marital relationship, more in small ways than anything major. Mainly the conflicts between my mom and I disturbed my husband, Dan. He always tried to smooth things over between us. My mom, always tough, wanted things her way and always believed she was right. I, being somewhat the same way, often clashed with her.

During her hospital stays before the stroke ever happened, Dan understood that I had to be there with her. He also felt bad because he knew I still had to work and carry on with my life. I just tried to squeeze as much into one twenty-four hour period as I could.

Dan and I made an agreement when we married. We agreed to take care of each other, and each of us was serious about honoring that agreement. When my mom had her stroke and ended up in the nursing home, I was an emotional wreck. There wasn't too much that Dan could do to help me. Hugs, our staple for most situations, only served as a reminder of what I had lost and what I had facing me. Because of everything that was going on with my mother, Dan became very agitated. At first, it confused me. I couldn't understand why he was complicating my already too complicated life. Finally, we both realized what was going on. Dan couldn't fix the situation, nor could he save me or protect me from it. This bothered him. He wasn't used to being in a position where he was helpless to give me comfort. At this point we agreed that love and understanding, a shoulder to cry on, and a few hugs were the only way that we were going to get through it. There were some rough spots, but mostly it worked.

Dan "nursed" me through the tough times. He listened to my pain, felt it, comforted me, and did what he could to help me through. He couldn't fix it—no one could—but he did everything else.

> *Your spouse or significant other is the most important person in your support system. Their support helps you maintain an equilibrium so that you can stay strong enough to be there for your parent. These times may try your relationship. Stand together and remain strong.*

## Negative Support

After my mom's stroke and during her early days in the nursing home, I received many suggestions from family members. Some of it was welcome and appreciated. Some of it was barely tolerated.

My youngest brother, who didn't seem particularly concerned after Mom's stroke, wrote me a letter. It strongly suggested that I do certain things regarding Mother, including getting her back to her own apartment. He sent copies of the letter to several other family members. The general tone implied that he knew what he was talking about and that I should listen.

He had only talked to her for ten minutes before making these recommendations! He had no idea of the severity of her stroke or the progress of her recovery. He didn't know about the diapers, or the inability to get up, or any of the other complications that made what he said impossible.

I replied with a scathing letter. I felt a little vulnerable myself and insecure with the decisions I had to make. But for him to come across as an authority totally infuriated me. Sometimes members of your family always see you as the little kid you once were.

My oldest brother, who had received a copy of my letter, wrote and said that maybe I was being a little too sensitive and I should cut that person some slack. Perhaps he was right, but he wasn't the one preached to by someone who didn't have a clue of the situation. That person would not have written him such a letter—which was my whole point. The whole situation made me want to scream, "I'm not eleven years old anymore!!"

*Wait before you respond to any negative or stupid suggestions regarding your parent. It may be ridiculous or uncalled for, but you're probably extra sensitive right now. (Do what I say, not what I did!)*

Passive Support

My husband, Dan, is a wonderful listener, and I talked and talked about everything that was going on concerning my mother. However, I needed more. I am a person who is more comfortable with the written word than the spoken word. That's where email stepped in. Thank goodness for computers. I could sit down at the computer and in a few minutes type out all the anxiety I'd been feeling. Press send, and hopefully I would soon receive some written commiseration.

Some people I would give almost daily updates on what was happening and how I was feeling about it. Other people that I didn't communicate with regularly would get a longer letter that included a broader span of time. Each letter helped me get through what I felt and what I had to deal with. The short letters were kind of a running account of "life with Mother," and the longer ones put everything into perspective.

These letters were very cathartic for me. Basically, I poured my heart out, which helped with the stress that I felt. Getting something "off your chest" is often the best way to deal with it. I needed to write these letters, and any commiserating reply that I received was just gravy.

I didn't start writing my "Mom" journal until almost a year past when my mom had her stroke. But all the emails that I sent were like keeping a journal. Luckily I kept them and saved a written record of the different happenings and my reactions to them.

> *You not only need someone to talk to, you need to write your feelings down. The very act of writing is beneficial to your mental health. If you don't have someone to write to, at the very least you should keep a journal. Write down not only what happens with your parent, but how you feel about it.*

## Permission Granted

When my mom first went into the hospital, I visited her every day. During her early days in the nursing home, I tried to visit her every day. I mentioned this to a friend who had lost her folks a few years before. She told me that it was nice that I went to see her all the time, but that my mother had nurses and other people who took care of her.

Not going every day wasn't an option. My mother didn't just demand my presence in words, she would manipulate me in whatever way she could. She had guilt down to a fine science. One time I called her because I couldn't make it to see her that day. She went on and on about how good she felt when I came to see her and how bad she felt when I didn't. How could I not go?

When I explained this to my friend, she told me about her experience. Her mother also demanded constant attention. She said that her mother's attempts at control and manipulation almost ruined her marriage. She said that our parents can't have control of us all the time, and it was important for me to take back control of my own life.

At about the same time, my sister-in-law, Ellen, shared her wisdom with me. "You do not need to spend hours every day with your mother," she told me. "Visit only once every three days. You do not need to stand in the path of her arrows and poison darts. Sacrificing your marriage or risking your sanity, would not help anybody," she said, "including your mother."

Both people made sense. Implementing their suggestions took more than courage, though. Standing up to my mother, even while she was lying on her back, took something that only she could give me: her own advice. Many times in years past, my mom had always told me, "Look out for number one, because no one else will." Looking out for number one, me, meant spending less time with my mother and more time living my own life.

> Don't abandon your parent, but at the same time don't abandon your own life. You know in an airplane, during the pre-flight instructions how they always say that if the oxygen masks drop down, always put on your own mask before putting on your child's mask? In that same way, always take care of yourself first. If you're not physically and mentally healthy, you'll be in no condition to take care of your parent.

## Looking Out for Number One

The first Christmas after Mom's stroke, I received a note from a long time friend. He had already been through what he called the "parental crisis", and he talked about family members revealing themselves. How right he was! Never before had the essence of a person come across so clearly as during these trials. Hints of who they really were may have been present before, but never so obvious.

My sister-in-law, Ellen, definitely gets the most supportive family member award. She counseled and supported me when I needed it the most, as well as wrote to my mother at least once a week the entire time she lived in the nursing home. She said she knew how important it was for people in that situation to have contact from the outside.

A cousin, many years out of touch and only recently reacquainted, was tremendously supportive to me and my mother. She visited when she could and helped me through the entire initial crisis. Often her support was like a warm ray of sunshine in an otherwise dark night. Her brother, living across the country, also helped tremendously. He had taken care of their mother in her later years and had many helpful suggestions. Any support, words of encouragement, or advice offered but not insisted upon, are really needed as you go through these trials.

Other family members were less than supportive. While some sent along messages of good cheer when Mom first had the stroke, they soon left thoughts of her behind. They went on with their busy lives, and I was left to deal with the fallout by myself.

What surprised me most is how most everyone wrote my mother off and essentially abandoned her shortly after she had her stroke. At first, everyone called with concern. But that didn't last. While I know that not everyone had the time or the resources to jump on a plane when the stroke happened, I thought that in the many months following it, they could find the time to get away. Barring that, they could have at least called or sent letters—neither of which is time or money intensive. But there were few calls and even fewer letters.

I asked a friend who was going through the same general situation as I was, if she felt resentful. When she answered no, it puzzled me for a long time. Was I a bad person for feeling resentful? Then it dawned on me: she was an only child! My feelings of resentment weren't directed toward my mother, which is what I thought, they were directed toward my invisible family members who left me in the lurch and left my mother forsaken.

*In these times of parental crisis, family members will reveal themselves to you. Be thankful of the support you get. Be ready for the surprises and then accept them. Now more than ever, you can't change people. Accept who they are and move on.*

Wake-up Call
I had lunch with a friend one day and discussed the mother situation once again. We had already covered it many times before. This time my friend told me something that changed my whole view of my mother.

She said, "I always used to make excuses for my mother, too." Until that point, I never realized that I was making excuses. I felt my mother had many reasons for doing what she did, and that's how I justified her actions—even if they were bad actions.

My friend was the unloved middle child and her mother treated her badly her whole life. My mother spoiled me rotten because I was the only girl and her obvious favorite. She supported me on my wild adventures, my wild animal pets, and my wild ideas. There was a lot about her that was positive, supportive, and loving, which made me feel guilty when I talked about the bad things.

Although she had many reasons for being like she was, it still didn't change the fact that she was an unpleasant and disagreeable woman who made everyone around her miserable. Well, not everyone. Some people found my mother delightful. It depended on who you were, how you dressed, and what your credentials were. If you were just a nurse who did your job and minded your own business, my mother would treat you like a servant, give orders, and display her rudeness. She was nice to her favorites, though. If you were a "professional," my mother would treat you with the utmost respect—basically like an equal. With me, she not only treated me like a servant, but if I didn't deliver she would not hesitate to disparage me. During my life she never hesitated to point out when I disappointed her.

My mother didn't deliberately hurt me. She loved me with all her heart. I always use this analogy: if you run someone over with your car and it was an accident, they're still dead whether you meant to do it or not. She didn't mean to hurt me, but the damage was still done.

When I was in high school, she had a meeting with my favorite teacher. I talked to him the next day and his question was, "How do you feel about your mother saying that you are all she has to live for?" What a thing to have to live with! How could I ever measure up? Despite her support, she let me know in so many little ways that I did not measure up. No wonder I had self-esteem problems.

After many years, I finally accepted who my mother really was and how she treated me. She may have brought me up in a way that caused self-esteem issues, but she also gave me the strength to overcome them. She may have been primarily negative, but there were also positive things about her. I had to learn from the negative and enjoy the positive. The important thing for me was to forgive her.

> *During these times with your parent, faults may be discovered or magnified. Faults you may not have seen or didn't want to see become too obvious to ignore. Accept them and forgive them. It's way too late to change them now. Learn from them and don't make the same mistakes. That's your parent's gift to you.*

### One Hundred Days

My mother didn't always mention when she talked to someone on the phone. So I was shocked to hear when my brother mentioned that it had been over one hundred days since he'd spoken to her. Because he lived in another country, he couldn't make outgoing phone calls because of the excessive cost. Apparently he had told Mother that she needed to get a phone card in order to call him. Unfortunately, Mother was in no position to understand the concept or convey the message to me. She might have been if I had walked in as they got off the phone, or even if the subject had come up in conversation. But neither of those events occurred. He assumed that I had gotten the message and was just refusing to get the cards for her.

Once I found out about the phone cards, I immediately purchased them and he and my mother communicated regularly. A miscommunication like this is probably common under these circumstances. I probably wouldn't have even mentioned it except that not all things are as they appear.

A few months after these events, it was Mother's Day. A couple weeks following that was my mother's birthday. You would think that someone who would count the days between phone conversations would at least send a card for those two holidays. Phone calls may be expensive, but postage is cheap. No cards arrived. The expense was just an excuse, and the hundred days just a graphic way of complaining.

>Some people who say the right
>things aren't necessarily going to do the
>right things. Some people who should
>be there for your parent might not be.
>When you expect other people to live up
>to who you think they are, you might be
>disappointed. If your parent would
>forgive these people, then you should,
>too. You probably should anyway.
>They're doing the best they can, just like
>you are.

## The Old Gray Mare Ain't What She Used to Be

Since I was the one closest to Mother and the one handling everything concerning her, it was my responsibility to disseminate all relevant information to family members. I tried to do this via email. Because I lived in a different time zone and was on a different schedule from everyone else, phone calls were difficult. With email, I could send more details to more people in a shorter amount of time.

My youngest brother came to visit her after she had been at the nursing home for over six months. In a letter he wrote after his visit, he said that although he brought his camera, he never took it out of the bag. He said there was nothing there that he wanted to remember. Although he applauded the virtues of the place where she lived by praising the patient and attentive staff, and the cleanliness and beauty of the surroundings, he had nothing positive to say about my mother.

Did he think he'd see the old mom with no consequences from the stroke? Why did he think that she'd been in a nursing home all that time? What he saw was reality. What he saw was what I had been living with and through for many months—and writing about. He finally saw the limitations of her body and her mind. It may have been sad and depressing, but it shouldn't have come as a surprise. I had sent many letters describing her failing eyesight (she didn't recognize him), her mobility in the wheelchair (she couldn't walk by herself), and her weaknesses (she fell asleep while he was visiting). Her general health, her condition, and her cognitive difficulties were no secret.

I thought I had covered everything in my emails. Every major or minor event including physical and cognitive challenges, I wrote about. I reported every time any health condition came up. Each time she had any kind of significant episode, or if I had one with her, I presented all the details.

Sometimes when one has an image in their mind of a person, an image developed over many years, it's difficult to let that image go, even though the person doesn't fit the image anymore. The old image may be comforting and the new details disturbing. It's not difficult to ignore the facts for more pleasant thoughts. But denying the facts doesn't alter the truth. I don't know if my letters inadequately explained the situation or if my brother chose happier thoughts. Whatever it was caused much sadness and grief.

*The person most in touch with the parent's situation should share all information with other family members. Give detailed and specific accounts of all aspects of the parent's new life. Don't leave out the bad things! They need to know the bad as well as the good. If someone is in denial of your parent's decline, don't try to force-feed them the truth. They will have to deal with it in their own time.*

Friends, Lovers, and Others
The most important support I received for the entire time my mother spent in the nursing home was the everyday kind: from my husband and from friends who I would hear from almost every day via phone or email. I would give them reports on what was going on and they would respond. Many times their responses were just a sentence or two, but it always felt like the right sentence at the right time. A word or two of praise, of comfort, or of commiseration as needed, always made me feel better.

I would complain of a tension headache, and someone would say, "No wonder you have a headache! Look at what you're going through!" Or I would lament about my mother saying something nasty to me, and someone would say, "You know she can't understand what's happening and she is confused," and I would be comforted. Sometimes they would just say that I was doing a good job and making the right decisions. There was no one else to say those things. My mother didn't realize I was doing a good job, and my family didn't appreciate the good job I was doing. These friends stood by me from the beginning of the nightmare to the end—virtually holding my hand, propping me up, or sharing my pain.

Another important form of support came from the nursing home itself: the social worker and the activities director. I can't guarantee that all social workers or activities directors are as wonderful or supportive as the ones that I experienced. But I can say that you need to give them a chance to help you. Because I'm shy, I wasn't able to converse easily with the social worker at first, and because of that, I probably lost a lot more support I might have received.

Between the two of them, they shared personal information about their families that made me feel that my problems weren't unique or insurmountable. My mother would often berate me and make me feel bad. The activities director commented on what a great relationship we had, and how proud my mother is of me and how happy she is with all I've done for her. That shocked me! My mother never expressed those sentiments to me! It took someone else to convey my mother's true feelings toward me. That's support.

*Your most important support will come from your significant other and from those friends you converse with on a daily basis. Also, give the nursing home staff a chance at helping with your support. They have the experience to know what to say to make you feel better. And sometimes feeling better is all you need.*

## The Rest of the Story

My niece, Amy, was always close to her grandmother. Mom taught her to sew, and as Amy grew up they had always spent many happy hours together.

After my mom's stroke, I became disappointed and disillusioned by Amy's actions. Amy had called to find out how everything was, but aside from a few inquiring emails, neither I nor my mother heard from her. She abandoned my mother and I felt sick and disgusted from that. It bothered me that Amy never even made an effort to call her grandmother after they had been so close for so long. I couldn't have been more wrong.

When Amy came to visit, I told her how disappointed I was that she never called her grandmother. She asked me how I knew if she had called or not. I told her that my mother had never mentioned it. Oops. As soon as I said it, I realized how stupid it sounded, and how stupid I was to think I could rely on a woman who couldn't even remember her roommate's name.

How easily misconceptions can occur. Amy also told me how she hated it when I sent her an email saying that her grandmother had fallen. She said that she always wished that I had written more details, but she didn't think it was right to ask. My interpretation was that she didn't ask because she didn't care. Boy, was I far off!

During our long talk, Amy also related to me a distressing incident. She had called my mother and for some reason, she thought Amy was somebody else. Amy said when she got off the phone she couldn't stop crying. I remember one time I had been talking to my mother about my aunt, and suddenly she thought she was talking to my aunt. I raised my voice trying to explain, in the same senseless way that people sometimes raised their voice when speaking to someone from another country, as if that would help. Finally I got off the phone, hurt and frustrated. But my hurt only lasted until the next time my mother was fine, which was probably the next day. Poor Amy probably thought that was how her grandmother had become—permanently.

When Amy and her family visited here, she spent time with my mother every day. She and her family ate lunch with her several times, and my mother enjoyed all the companionship. Everything I had thought about Amy, every bad thought, every disappointing notion, had been incorrect. Amy came through in a big way, and contrary to my original assumptions, she had not abandoned my mother at all.

*Before you are hurt or disappointed by various family members seeming inactions regarding your parent, make sure your assumptions are correct.*

*Sometimes making judgments without having all the facts hurts everyone involved.*

\* \* \* \* \*

Points to Remember:

1. There are many types of support, and during these trying times, you will need them all. Sometimes, those who you expected to be most supportive won't be. And sometimes, someone you never expected to be supportive at all, will step forward to help. Never say no to any support that is offered.

2. Anyone can have a debilitating stroke or some other devastating thing happen. A Power of Attorney (both financial and medical) should be as mandatory as a will. If you will not be the designee, find someone trustworthy. Different states have different rules regarding these documents.

3. If you have the Power of Attorney, or if you are responsible for making decisions like this, remember that your parent's well-being is the most important thing to consider. Ignore the pressure and do what's right, or as my other used to say, "Follow your heart."

4. Your spouse or significant other is the most important person in your support system. Their support helps you maintain an equilibrium so that you can stay strong enough to be there for your parent. These times may try your relationship. Stand together and remain strong.

5. Wait before you respond to any negative or stupid suggestions regarding your parent. It may be ridiculous or uncalled for, but you're probably extra sensitive right now. (Do what I say, not what I did!)

6. You not only need someone to talk to, you need to write your feelings down. The very act of writing is beneficial to your mental health. If you don't have someone to write to, at the very least you should keep a journal. Write down not only what happens with your parent, but how you feel about it.

7. Don't abandon your parent, but at the same time don't abandon your own life. You know in an airplane, during the pre-flight instructions how they always say that if the oxygen masks drop down, always put on your own mask before putting on your child's mask? In that same way, always take care of yourself first. If you're not physically and mentally healthy, you'll be in no condition to take care of your parent.

8. In these times of parental crisis, family members will reveal themselves to you. Be thankful of the support you get. Be ready for the surprises and then accept them. Now more than ever, you can't change people. Accept who they are and move on.

9. During these times with your parent, faults may be discovered or magnified. Faults you may not have seen or didn't want to see become too obvious to ignore. Accept them and forgive them. It's way too late to change them now. Learn from them and don't make the same mistakes. That's your parent's gift to you.

10. Some people who say the right things aren't necessarily going to do the right things. Some people who should be there for your parent,

might not be. When you expect other people to live up to who you think they are, you might be disappointed. If your parent would forgive these people, then you should, too. You probably should anyway. They're doing the best they can, just like you are.

11. The person most in touch with the parent's situation should share all information with other family members. Give detailed and specific accounts of all aspects of the parent's new life. Don't leave out the bad things! They need to know the bad as well as the good. If someone is in denial of your parent's decline, don't try to force-feed them the truth. They will have to deal with it in their own time.

12. Your most important support will come from your significant other and from those friends you converse with on a daily basis. Also, give the nursing home staff a chance at helping with your support. They have the experience to know what to say to make you feel better. And sometimes feeling better is all you need.

13. Before you are hurt or disappointed by various family members seeming inactions regarding your parent, make sure your assumptions are correct. Sometimes making judgements without having all the facts hurt everyone involved.

*Excerpt from a Friend's Email:*
*I don't know how you are making all these decisions alone right now. No wonder your head hurts. But when you say that your mother is happy and doing well, then the decisions you are making must be the right ones as difficult as they seem. I think you are doing a great job of being there for your mom, and it really is okay for you not to do*

everything. I've said it before, but she is really lucky to have you there for her. You have nothing to be guilty about...you are and have been a wonderful daughter.

## Chapter 4
## Emotions and Revelations: The Guilt Will Eat You Alive

A Matter of Perspective

Two of my brothers felt that my mother was better off dead. They thought her quality of life sucked, that she wasn't capable of enjoying life, that her money could be better spent elsewhere, and that she should die. They wrote letters itemizing everything I was doing wrong and how bad my choices were. I spent many hours agonizing over their accusations and wondering if I was making the correct choices.

When I shared the letters with my husband and my friends, they all defended my position. They talked about how the letters were written by greedy, bitter, selfish, and heartless people. Their comments made me feel better but I still had some doubts about the correctness of my decisions regarding my mother.

A few days after this happened, I had to attend a Quarterly Care Meeting at the nursing home. What a pleasant surprise and a revelation that turned out to be. Everyone there enjoyed her and thought she had a great sense of humor. The main chef who ran the kitchen said she was the first one in the dining room every morning, and he looked forward to talking with her because she was such a treat. Another person talked about how much she appreciated spending time with my mom because she learned so much from her. These were much different comments than the ones I read in those terrible letters! It was like they were talking about a different person.

That's when I realized the truth of the situation. My two brothers who wrote the letters did not know my mother. The people from the nursing home knew her very well—perhaps even better than I did. They spent far more time with her than anyone else did. My brothers had spent four hours with her in almost two years. They didn't know her; they only thought they knew her. What they knew was four hours out of many thousands of hours. During that time if she was tired, or sick, or in the midst of one of her many strokes, they would receive distorted impressions. My brothers made their comments and disparaged me based on information so limited it was insignificant.

When I had a private conversation with the social worker at the nursing home, it surprised her that my brothers requested no drugs or hospitalization. She said, "Your mother will probably get to that point eventually, but she's not there yet. She's still full of life!"

At 3:30 one morning not long after the insulting letters, I received a call that my mother had to go to the hospital. The nurse said she was having trouble breathing and she was scared. The ambulance was about to pick her up. When I got off the phone, my husband said, "What are you supposed to say? No, don't take her?" I laughed at his reference to the letters saying that she shouldn't be allowed to go to the hospital. What would they have said when they received the call?

"Give her two aspirin and call me in the morning?" The thought of not letting her go to the hospital was absurd.

While at the hospital she delighted all the nurses as usual. She recovered quickly and returned to the nursing home where she continued enjoying life and entertaining others; much to the chagrin of certain whiny family members who had other plans for her and her money.

> *Don't think your family is immune from indiscretions. If money is involved, you'd be surprised what people can turn into. Even people you thought you knew sometimes turn into monsters right before your eyes. Also, family members who don't have the entire picture may suggest inappropriate actions.*

<u>Partly Cloudy or Mostly Sunny?</u>
It had been many months since my mother entered the nursing home and I had dutifully visited her at least twice a week right from the start. Not only did I dread going to see her, I felt guilty about dreading it. The conflict between what I did and not wanting to do it affected me badly. I was a guilt-ridden mess. I remember a letter I wrote to a friend during this time. In it, I asked her if I was a bad daughter for not wanting to do the things I did for her. Or, I wondered, was I a good daughter for doing them even though I really didn't want to? Not understanding where these feelings came from confused me even more.

Shortly after that, I had to deal with a distasteful incident that my mother had provoked. I found myself in the social worker's office. Like so many times my mother sat in the vice-principal's office defending me when I was in high school, I sat there trying to make amends for her actions. This was definitely a case of role reversal! Frankly, I was afraid that they might want to kick my mother out for her poor behavior! Instead of scolding me for my mother's actions, the social worker was understanding. In fact, what she said to me that afternoon changed my point of view and affected my life. If you are lucky enough to have a compassionate social worker who not only looks after your parent's feelings, but yours as well, consider yourself fortunate.

Gloria said, "You know, your mom reminds me of my grandmother. I hope you don't mind me saying this." "No," I said as I hung on every word. Gloria continued, "My grandmother always thought she was this happy person who got along with everybody. And as long as she didn't open her mouth, it might have been true. But as soon as you turned up the sound, it was all negativity. She made everyone around her miserable."

Wow! With that enlightening conversation, it was like taking off a heavy, cumbersome coat. All this weight I had been dragging around for months was gone. No wonder no one wanted to be her roommate! No wonder I had to force myself to come visit for so long! That conversation validated everything I felt.

My mother had always been a "glass half empty" person, but I had only recently begun to realize it. I was still absorbing the reality of that. She was critical and demanding, and she complained about everything. Although the guilt didn't go away completely, Gloria not only helped to reduce it, but she helped me to understand myself and my mother better.

*If you're going through guilt or any other emotional ordeal, talk to the social worker of the nursing home. If your parent is at home, talk to a professional experienced in elder caretaking.*

Pull My Strings

As my mother began to regain her strength, she also became more demanding. She thought she could do things that she just couldn't do. The damage from the stroke impaired her judgment about her abilities.

One day I came to visit, and she was on her bed wanting to get into her wheelchair. My mother thought all she needed was a hand to support her and she could get up by herself. I knew it wasn't as simple as that, but there was no convincing her. During recent visits I had always seen two nurses helping her up and I tried to explain that to her. Also, I told her that if I had to do it myself I could hurt my back. Later when I was getting ready to leave, she didn't want me to. She wanted me to stay until dinner.

When a nurse came in my mother immediately launched into this agitated tirade about me hurting my back and having to get home to my husband along with other insulting comments about me. It felt taunting and deliberate. As I walked out, I heard the nurse tell her that she needed to get a second person to help get my mother into the wheelchair.

While driving home, I was furious with what she had said and how she had made me feel. I kept thinking that I wouldn't call her or go to see her all week. What is determined in anger is often reversed in guilt.

The following day I called her. She immediately thanked me for calling and told me how good she felt when I came to see her and how important my visits were to her. I tried to explain that I couldn't come every day but she wouldn't let up. Instead of cutting down on my visits, she compelled me to come more often.

Her taunting me the day before, and the following day saying how good my visits made her feel, were related. It took me a long time to figure this out, but it was all manipulation. She knew I was angry about the previous day so she used guilt to reel me back in. Although I feel embarrassed that it took me so long to realize what was going on, I do understand that I was blinded by emotion at the time.

*If you're having strong emotional reactions to what is going on with your parent, examine the situation to see if your parent is somehow eliciting that response. It's better for both of you if you discover this action before it becomes a habit.*

<u>A Tale of Two Daughters</u>
At the same time I was going through turmoil and emotional upheaval with my mother, I had a friend in a similar situation. Although my mother lived in a nursing home, her mother lived in a house across the street from her.

We would discuss different aspects of our parents' decline. When my mother demanded that I take her for a ride and I didn't want to but had such guilt feelings about it, I discussed it with my friend. I told her that it concerned me that my mother didn't always make it to the toilet, and I didn't want to deal with that in my car.

Her take on it was so different that it shocked me and made me feel ashamed. She said that her mother wore an incontinent pad, too, just like my mother. But she added that whenever they go anyplace, she just brings along extra pads, another set of clothes, and a towel. She sounded so matter-of-fact about it like it was nothing. To me the whole idea of taking her in my car was monumental.

I thought that talking to this friend about similar problems would make me feel better. Instead, it made me feel much worse. A cousin of mine whose husband had had a stroke called me. I told her the whole sad tale of how I was a failure as a good daughter. She made many comments that made sense to me.

The first thing that she said was that you can only do what you can do. Different people can do different things, and you can't get down on yourself for the things that you're not comfortable doing. She said that my friend and I are different people, and although the situation is the same, the rest of it is different. It wasn't fair to compare myself to her and the way she handled the situation.

Several months later as proof that my cousin's advice exposed the truth, this same friend said that she admired me for the way I handled my entire mother situation. She meant it, too. And I answered back that I admired her for the way she handled her entire mother situation. And I meant it, too.

Remember that different people can handle and can do different things. Your background is different, and although the situation may appear the same, it usually isn't. Just do what you can do and don't compare yourself with others.

## Old Memories, Sad Memories

One day on the way to work I heard a commercial for a nursing home. It provoked such intense sadness in me that tears came to my eyes. I realized that long after my mother's death, I could never hear such a commercial without being profoundly affected.

Now and then I come across something of hers in my house, and it always makes me feel sad. Sometimes just finding a recipe in her writing can bring me to tears. Seeing a book by an author she liked, smelling a perfume that she wore, or even seeing a television show that she used to watch always had an emotional effect on me.

Even before she died, all of those things bothered me. They symbolized the mom that was already gone instead of the mother that came to be.

*Hearing, seeing, or smelling anything that reminds you of your parent will never again be easy. Those things are a constant reminder of what you have lost.*

## Beach Boy

It's only in retrospect that I realize how much of my anxiety was caused from defending and protecting my mother from the slights of others. Sometimes family members who you think should feel close to your parent and act that way, just don't. They may have their own reasons, their own demons, or their own excuses. Sometimes it is difficult to deal with; especially when it's happening and before you can look at it objectively.

After my mother broke her wrist, I sent out an email to all appropriate family members. This was one response that I received: "Thanks for the information. I hope things go well for her. I'm about to spend three days at the beach with my friends." If that rebuff wasn't enough, two days later I received this email: "My beach trip has been canceled. What's her number?"

Oh my goodness! Didn't he realize how blatantly cold and uncaring those two exchanges sounded? It took my husband days to calm me after I received those two emails. I was walking around and spewing obscenities for a week! Could that man be any more of a jerk?

Not too long after that, my mother told me that she had talked to him. He told her that he was coming to America to visit (he lived in a foreign country), but he didn't think that he would be able to see her. What! Traveling over ten thousand miles and you can't come an extra two hundred miles to see your mother who may not last through the year? His lack of consideration astounded me so much, that I didn't say a word.

My mother never knew about the two irreverent emails. And she did not react to him saying that he couldn't come to visit her. I honestly think that she didn't comprehend the enormity of it—that he lived so far and would be so close. But it also could have been her emotional brick wall that protected her from insults and rejections through the years. I asked her if it bothered her and she responded, "No, it's okay. He has more important things to do."

> There will be times when you cannot protect your parent from slights and disregard of others. Most times there is nothing you can do, so don't let it get to you. Your parent would probably forgive them anyway, so you should, too.

## To Visit or Not to Visit

The person described above, my youngest brother, did eventually make the effort to visit my mother. He spent a painful two hours with her. Clearly, what he saw emotionally devastated him. Although I had sent detailed emails describing my mother's mental and physical health, when he talked to her on the phone and her voice sounded so normal, he must have forgotten her true condition. After he returned home, he wrote a sad letter about how he found her.

The letter would not have made such an impact on me except that he sent it to my oldest brother who was considering coming to visit. When I didn't hear from him for a while after he received the letter, I feared he had taken the words to heart and had decided not to visit.

Writing to ask if he was reconsidering his trip because of what he'd read, I tried to explain the letter was based on just two hours in one day. Our mother was not always the way he had described her. There were times when, if you could ignore the wheelchair, you would think you were talking to the mother of three years ago (prior to her stroke). The operative words were, "there were times." Sometimes she was as described in the letter, a pitiful old woman. And sometimes she was as we remember her, spunky and full of life. Most of the time she was just in between.

I told him that our mother was not always the gross individual that had been described. She was not the same mother as before her stroke, and if someone expected that, then they might have the same reaction as my youngest brother. But if you could accept that this is a different person, in a different body, with different needs and a different reality, then you could handle it.

As it turned out, the letter had nothing to do with not hearing from him, and he and his wife did come out for a visit with our mother. Mother enjoyed it tremendously, and although they saw her on good days and bad days, there were no surprises.

*If someone has not seen your parent for some time, make sure they know what to expect so there will not be any surprises. Those kinds of surprises are not good for anyone.*

<u>Quality of Life</u>

More times over the years than I could ever count, my mother told me to "give her a push" if she ever became incapacitated. One time shortly before her stroke when I took her to the hospital emergency room for a congestive heart episode, she even told the doctor who treated her that she never wanted to live like that. She told him that she didn't want to waste money to stay alive if she wasn't whole.

Although I knew I could never do what she asked, I always told her that I would take care of it.

Part of me always thought the situation would never come up. No kid wants to think about the mortality of their parent—even a fifty-year-old kid.

After her stroke when she became what she had wanted me to prevent, I was unprepared for my feelings and for her new persona. Though I couldn't grant her wishes, I did accept them. What I never expected was how much the new mother embraced life.

The old, original mom would want us to get rid of the new "partial" mother. But the new mother wanted to live. She loved playing and winning bingo, she loved the compliments on her clothes, she even loved complaining and being demanding. The new mother, while not the same person as the old mom, didn't care about the quality of her life. To her, it was a good life. She may have liked to complain, but mostly she was having good time.

The new mother didn't remember the old mom. The new mother didn't remember that she never wanted to be like that. The new mother didn't want to die.

But if the old mom saw this new mother, she would be furious. I can picture the rage in her eyes, her finger waving in the air, and her words spilling out in an angry profusion. "I **TOLD** you to take care of this! Look at me! I never wanted this!" The scorn and disdain in her voice. That look that cuts right through you. I can see it, picture it, feel it.

And yet here is the new mother, her face lighting up as she shows me her latest winnings at bingo, and tells me of all the compliments she's gotten that day. The new mother who doesn't have a clue of what she has become.

She loved her bingo. Was that enough? She still got joy out of life. Maybe not as much joy as I would have wished for my mother, but it seemed to be enough for her. Who is the one who decides what quality of life is? Is it my perception of quality of life, or is it hers? Which one is the true quality of life and which one matters?

Your parent's life is his or her own. What you think of the quality of their existence may not be what they think about it. Many parents in a nursing home don't know or don't remember what they were like before. So their perspective of their life is different from yours. And that's a good thing.

<u>What a Day!</u>
The day started with my mother calling to tell me that her clock wasn't working again. She said it wasn't working the night before and it wasn't working a couple hours ago. Now, it's fine, though. How can an electric clock not work sometimes and work perfectly at other times? It can't. Even the simplest concepts often elude her.

That afternoon when I came to see her, I brought her some oranges and grapefruit that she had been asking for. When I gave them to her she said, "Boy, I really wanted one last night." Nothing I did for her seemed to be enough. Even when I did something kind for her, she would turn it around and make me feel bad about it. She had a knack for making you feel like you did something wrong even when you did something right. Negative reinforcement.

Before too much longer in the visit she hit me with something else. She said, "Can't you wear a nicer pair of jeans than that?" I said, "They're brand new jeans!" And they were. She said, "Why can't you wear pants made out of material like this," and she pointed to her own slacks. I said, "Because I don't wear pants like that." She said, "You have loved wearing jeans ever since you were a little girl." This was just another one of the radical contrasts between my mother and me. She loved clothes and loved dressing up. I loved my jeans.

As I left there, I breathed easier knowing that I didn't have to see her again for four days. It was just so taxing and depressing and guilt producing. She always made me feel inadequate and like I disappointed her. She made me feel bad about myself.

> *To paraphrase a great novelist, these are the best of times, these are the worst of times. Some days are worse than others. Try to make the best of them.*

## Bosom Buddy

My mother and I were always close. I confided in her all the time and told her almost every detail about my life. After her stroke, it was difficult getting used to not being able to do that anymore.

I would still gravitate toward telling her some problem before I realized that it was as inappropriate as telling it to a five-year-old. It's just that she was so much like my "real mom" that I'd forget that she wasn't whole.

For so many years, she was the one I went to with all my problems. She didn't always give me the right answer and she didn't always give me the answer I wanted to hear. But she was always there for me, always listened, and always tried to help with her advice. It was difficult not having her there anymore.

Besides "accidentally" sharing problems with her, I would also consult her about financial matters. Unfortunately, I did that much longer than I should have without realizing that it was a grave error. It wasn't good for me to depend on advice from someone who wasn't whole, and it wasn't good for her to struggle to come up with a solution for me.

*It's important to be aware of when to stop discussing important matters with your parent. Don't discuss concerns after the time that it becomes inappropriate to do so.*

## Mr. Spock, She's Not

My mother told me she had big beetles in her room. I listened half-heartedly because when she told me about the mouse it turned out to be the handle on the window. This time she said that she had found one under the bathroom door, trapped it under there, and killed it. When I went over to look at it, there was a deep hole in the linoleum. I said, "That's not a beetle!" She asked, "What is it, then?" I explained to her that it was a hole in the floor. She wanted me to get rid of it and wouldn't take no for an answer.

The conversation went on far longer than a rational conversation should have gone on. It was totally illogical. I could understand with her poor eyesight mistaking a hole in the floor for a beetle. But once she found out it was just a hole, she should have let it go. Instead, she still wanted me to get rid of the dead body. It bothered me that she was illogical so much of the time.

First I thought that it was difficult for me to accept how illogical she had become. Then I realized I was fooling myself. She had always been illogical but since her stroke, it had been about blatantly stupid subjects. An old boyfriend of mine used to send me into a rage over how illogical he was. I didn't realize how close to home it was. My mother used to make me angry, but I would try repeatedly and fruitlessly to show her the light. It was always futile. She knew she was right, no matter how wrong she was.

The Christmas before her stroke, we shared a wonderful Christmas dinner at our house. When it came time to take her home, she started talking about how we paid too much for our house. No matter what I said or what evidence I presented, she was certain her viewpoint was correct. I talked about its uniqueness, that someone else had already bid on the property, and how we were determined to own it. Nothing mattered. A beautiful Christmas day was ruined because she refused to be wrong. Another time we bought a very used car. We just needed a four-wheel drive car to get us through the winter. Although the car we bought was old, it ran perfectly. When I told her about the car and how much we paid for it, she said that it was probably only worth one hundred dollars. Not only was she illogical, but she was condescending at the same time.

*Sometimes you realize that a trait that you thought you had never seen before is actually just a tweaked version of one that had been there all along.*

Sometimes it takes a while to realize or acknowledge such traits in your parent.

Piling on the Guilt

One sultry afternoon my mother told me that she needed to go to a dentist. She wanted to know why she couldn't go to the one she went to last time. I reminded her that he was in Arizona. She said, "Oh! That's right!" Then she proceeded to tell me that she is thinking of moving back to Arizona because I don't do anything for her. "Like what?" I asked. She brought up coming to dinner on Sundays like she used to. When I mentioned that she would have a hard time using our bathroom because it didn't have support bars like the bathroom in the nursing home, she got angry. Then she said that she can stand up by herself and it wouldn't be a problem. From there, she immediately went back to the Arizona discussion, and she said she was concerned about the flight. I told her I'd be happy to arrange everything. The conversation fell apart from there and I left feeling terrible.

A few weeks later, I wheeled her past a television that showed two kayakers rowing smoothly by. "We'd like to get a couple of those," I said. She asked why we needed two. And I told her one for each of us. "And maybe one for our dog," I joked. Then she said, "And one for me. If I drown, I drown." Astonished, I said, "You don't care?" She answered, "If you don't care that I have sat here every day for the past year, and you never take me anywhere, then why should I care what happens to me?" Whew! That arrow went straight to the heart. Shortly after this happened, I took her for a ride and she wanted to come home when we were barely halfway through. The ride sounded like a good idea to her, but in actuality it was beyond her comfort level.

After not talking to my mother for a couple days, her first words to me on the phone were, "Where did we leave off?" Then she went on and on about what she wanted me to bring her and when could I come, and then mentioning a few jobs that she wanted me to do for her. When I told her that I couldn't come that day, the conversation abruptly ended. She suddenly said, "Okay, if you can't come then I have nothing else to say. Good-by." Dial tone. That leaves you feeling pretty empty.

>When your parent starts laying on the guilt, there's not much you can do. Get out of the way of it if you can. Or see if you can change the subject or even make a joke about it.

Sad Realization

When a parent has had a stroke or some other health problem that requires you to care for them, sometimes a realization hits you that astonishes you. Perhaps it is that your parent's faults seem magnified at times like this. Perhaps it is that with all the other stress involved, it just becomes clearer than it ever was before. Whatever it is that triggers the realization, it is never easy and it is always sad.

When I came to visit my mother one day she sat in the hallway talking with Bob. She and Bob had a hankering for some popcorn and she wanted me to get them some. When I told her there was nowhere around there to get it, she started getting pushy. She said, "Go to the corner and just get it!" With an edge to her voice, she just kept insisting. She went from pushy to disparaging to downright mean. But the worst part was that it felt "familiar."

This was not the first time she had talked to me like that. This was not the first time that she made me feel bad. But this was the first time that I put a label to it: this was abusive. Many times through the years she had made me feel guilty and manipulated me in various subtle ways. It was only now that I began to realize that if you added up all the little things, they added up to abuse.

My mother was abusive to me. Thinking that thought felt terrible. Writing it makes me feel even worse. To acknowledge that about a parent, and realizing how long you've lived with that abuse, and wondering what damage it has done over the years, is all too much to think about.

*Often with your parent in a nursing home or cared for at home, something will come to the surface that has been there all along. Sometimes these realizations can benefit you in many ways. Accept them for the gifts that they are.*

She Said, She Said

My mother called me one morning to say that I don't come to visit often enough. I asked her what would be enough? She answered that I should come twice a week like I used to. I tried to explain that I still came twice a week, but no matter what I said, she wouldn't listen. When we hung up the phone and I gave her my usual, "I love you," she responded with, "I wonder if you do ..."

Another time on the phone she asked when I was coming to visit. I told her Tuesday. She asked if tomorrow was Tuesday. I told her tomorrow was Monday. She told me that someone told her that today is Monday. I said, "No, today is Sunday." She insisted that they said it was Monday. I finally said, "Mom, do you think I am lying to you?" Her response was, "Do you think they are lying?" It felt like she argued with me constantly and doubted me all the time. She made me feel bad about myself.

*Sometimes it's better not to argue. If you can distract your parent with something else, that usually works best.*

### Black and Blue

Sometimes after the initial crisis fades, you don't realize how much your parental situation has impacted your life. With my husband and me, there seemed to be a low level of tension running through our lives no matter how smoothly everything appeared to be going. Every telephone call brought fear. Was it another call from the nursing home that something was wrong? Or even worse, was it another one of my mother's too frequent calls? Some were short and just amounted to her wanting some innocent information. Some were in the middle of the night when she was confused. Some were extremely upsetting when she accused me or someone else of some imagined infraction, or demanding to be taken home (to the nursing home) when that's where she already was. But most of them were just plain painful when she called continually to complain about something, demand something, or to tell me how I failed her. They usually caused me to feel bad about myself, which is why we dreaded them.

Shortly after my mother's stroke and subsequent transfer to the nursing home, I frequently had chest pains and headaches. As time went by, they eased off. But there were still bad times that brought them back. Often I would find that my breathing was so ragged that it scared me. I would have to slow down, relax, and attempt to think happy, stress-free thoughts. Sometimes it worked, sometimes it didn't.

One day when my husband and I were both upset about some inconceivably small incident, we came to realize how the whole caretaking situation had rubbed us raw. Even the normal bumps and bruises of life that are normally brushed off, now drew blood. Our emotions were so sensitive that it felt like any little thing could bring us down. Our awareness of that helped us to stop the bleeding.

*You never know how a caretaking situation is going to affect your life. Try to be cognizant of it and take care of yourself. Bring as much relaxation into your life as you can.*

Withdrawal
The day started dreadfully as my mother issued complaint after complaint over the phone. Most of the complaints were unjustified and annoying. It didn't make me happy about going to visit her. The visit turned out to be much worse than I could ever have imagined.

A short time before this occurred, she had started leaving her dirty clothes on a chair wanting me to check to make sure her name was on each item. Once in a while I would catch one that had no name, but usually each item was already marked. So on this day I went through a stack of clothes, most of which were destined for the dirty clothes. She wanted me to put the dirty clothes in the laundry slots outside, but I didn't know how to divide the clothes, so I refused to do that. Although she was angry, she let it go.

Next, I put away all the clothes piled on the bottom of her closet. Then I plucked all her chin hairs. After that, she wanted me to go through her nylon stockings to take home the dirty ones and wash them for her.

When I finished that, she wanted me to put some powder on her face for her. I am extremely sensitive to anything that has a fragrance, and most of my mother's cosmetics had strong fragrances. She knew I had problems with that, but when I told her that I'd put it on her right before I left, she still argued. Finally, I told her that I would put it on her whenever she wanted me to, but then I would have to leave immediately.

Then she asked if I could put on her rouge for her. I told her I could, but why didn't she consider to stop using make-up. She said she uses it because she looks so pretty when it's on. I told her she looked pretty without it on, too. After I put the rouge on, she wanted me to put on her lipstick, so I did that, too. She mentioned the powder and we went through that whole discussion again. As a compromise, she said that I could put the powder on her and then I could take her to the lunchroom.

As we were leaving (after putting on the powder), she started talking to a nurse who had walked into the room. My mother said to her, "My daughter wouldn't put on my powder because she says she's allergic to it." She said it offensively in an obvious effort to tick me off. It worked. But the nurse told her that it would make her sneeze, too. I squeezed my mother's shoulder and said, "See, I'm not the only one."

As we were about to go into the lunchroom, she said to me, "I didn't get good use out of you today," which infuriated me after all I had done that day. "Is that all I'm here for?" I asked. As I drove home, I had to do some deep breathing to calm myself down.

That night after I told my husband how she had taunted and belittled me, he thought that I shouldn't go see her for a week. My feeling was that not only was that a great idea, but I was still so angry that I didn't even want to talk to her for a few days. I disconnected our answering machine and didn't answer the phone for a couple days. She had pushed me too far this time.

The phone rang several times when I thought it might be her. I felt guilty about not answering, but I also felt free. I needed to look out for myself. The following day I answered her call but was in the middle of tending our woodstove and had to tell her that I'd call her back in five minutes. When she first heard my voice she said, "Hi . . .", like she hadn't heard from me in a while.

When I called her back, it was mostly complaints again, and I could hardly wait to get off the phone. She asked when I was coming to visit, and I told her in a few days. I had finally begun to stand up for myself and not put up with her abuse anymore. I decided I needed more protecting than she did. She was safe and warm and dry and not abused. Although I was safe and warm and dry, she abused me almost every day, and it was time to step back and not allow her to do that to me anymore.

The next time I spoke to her, she asked when I was coming to visit, and I told her Monday. She asked if I was skipping a day and I tried to get around that. Always knowing the right words to say to make me feel guilty, she said, "You know I'm terribly lonely here." I told her that I had a lot to do and she said that she knows that I have a life of my own. Finally she said, "Well, as long as you're doing the best that you can." She seemed to understand that things were changing.

The next day when she called, she went on and on about her clothes piling up on the chair. I told her I didn't know why she had started to pile them up like that instead of just putting them in the dirty clothes like she used to. She said that they had been building up because I hadn't been there in a long time. At that instant my oatmeal bell conveniently rang, and I told her I had to get off the phone. She said that I always get off the phone when she says something that I don't like. I told her that I get off the phone when she tries to make me feel guilty. My husband was impressed that she was sharp enough to pick that up at all.

About a week later on the phone, she asked if I was coming that day. I told her no, that I would be coming on Monday again. She said, "Oh, so you're only coming once a week now." I told her that was correct. She wanted to know why. After thinking about it, I told her because she made me feel bad. Her response was, "If you don't want me to call anymore, I won't." I said, "No, that's okay, you can call."

Although I didn't realize it at the time, her asking about not calling anymore was intended to make me feel guilty. Luckily, it just went past me. There weren't too many more comments about me cutting back on visiting. It was almost as though she knew it had to be that way. Ironically enough, or maybe not so ironically, we started getting along much better at that point. After that, she would only rarely taunt me or insult me. I think it was a power trip on her part. Once I took the power away from her, she settled down and "behaved."

*When you are driven to take what feels like drastic measures to keep the peace with your parent, that is often exactly what the situation calls for. The solution you come up with may feel harsh, but it is often better for everyone involved.*

Power Plays
One morning when my mother called me, she couldn't hear me. The noise in the background had been from the beginning of the call. It sounded like someone was moving something. Suddenly, my mother yelled, "Stop that! Can't you stop that while I'm on the phone! Stop that! I can't hear!" She said it rudely and aggressively. Although they had started moving the object before she dialed the phone, she thought it was perfectly in her rights to demand them to stop.
Another time I was on the phone with my mother and I heard a nurse come into the room and greet her. She responded by saying harshly, "Make this bed! I can't stand this mess!" The way she treated people bothered me. I hadn't realized how mean she was. I always made excuses for her because she had a hard emotional life. But many people have hard lives and they don't treat other people like that.

A nurse related a story to me that made me angry with my mother. She was in the bathroom one day when her roommate really had to go. Instead of being considerate and hurrying up for her, my mother took her time. And after she finished using the toilet, she stayed in there primping herself and fixing her hair while her roommate waited outside with her legs crossed. My mother loved to control people and situations and this was just another example.

What sounded like an injustice to my mother turned out to be another power play. She told me that she was coughing and the nurse wouldn't bring her any water. My first inclination was, "How dare they do that to my mom!", until I heard the rest of the story. Everyone knew that my mother had a chronic cough, and when she coughed she was not in any danger. While a nurse fed a patient in the bed across from hers, my mother started on one of her coughing jags which happened several times a day. She demanded a glass of water deliberately to try to get the nurse away from the other patient. It was just another power play. She wanted to be perceived as the most important person. When I heard these sad tales, I always figured that someday all her rantings, ravings, and demandings would eventually come back to haunt her.

My husband was concerned and felt bad about the possibility of my mother saying something mean to someone and what if that was their last day on earth. That would be so sad. I can't be sure, but I think it might have even happened. My mother ate lunch with a man who had a medical problem that he couldn't close his mouth, so it hung open. Every time she sat down with him, she would immediately start making fun of his open mouth. One time I brought her to lunch and he wasn't there, and I never saw him again. What a sad thing to happen.

*If your parent is at a nursing home or even a day care facility, you can't be watching them all the time. You cannot be responsible for their offensive behavior. In a way, they can be like little children not knowing that something is wrong to say or do. Make amends when you can.*

\* \* \* \* \*

Points to Remember:

1. Don't think your family is immune from indiscretions. If money is involved, you'd be surprised what people can turn into. Even people you thought you knew sometimes turn into monsters right before your eyes. Also, family members who don't have the entire picture may suggest inappropriate actions.

2. If you're going through guilt or any other emotional ordeal, talk to the social worker at the nursing home. If your parent is at home, talk to a professional experienced in elder caretaking.

3. If you're having strong emotional reactions to what is going on with your parent, examine the situation to see if your parent is somehow eliciting that response. It's better for both of you if you discover this action before it becomes a habit.

4. Remember that different people can handle and can do different things. Your background is different, and although the situation may appear the same, it usually isn't. Just do what you can do and don't compare yourself with others.

5. Hearing, seeing, or smelling anything that reminds you of your parent will never again be easy. Those things are a constant reminder of what you have lost.

6. There will be times that you cannot protect your parent from slights and disregard of others. Most times there is nothing you can do, so don't let it get to you. Your parent would probably forgive them anyway, so you should, too.

7. If someone has not seen your parent for some time, make sure they know what to expect so there will not be any surprises. Those kinds of surprises are not good for anyone.

8. Your parent's life is his or her own. What you think of the quality of their existence may not be what they think about it. Many parents in a nursing home don't know or don't remember what they were like before. So their perspective of their life is different from yours. And that's a good thing.

9. To paraphrase a great novelist, these are the best of times, these are the worst of times. Some days are worse than others. Try to make the best of them.

10. It's important to be aware of when to stop discussing important matters with your parent. Don't discuss concerns when it becomes inappropriate to do so.

11. Sometimes you realize that a trait that you thought you had never seen before is actually just a tweaked version of one that had been there all along. Sometimes it takes a while to realize or acknowledge such traits in your parent.

12. When your parent starts laying on the guilt, there's not much you can do. Get out of the way of it if you can. Or see if you can change the subject or even make a joke about it.

13. Often with your parent in a nursing home or cared for at home, something will come to the surface that has been there all along. Sometimes these realizations can benefit you in many ways. Accept them for the gifts that they are.

14. Sometimes it's better not to argue. If you can distract your parent with something else, that usually works best.

15. You never know how a caretaking situation is going to affect your life. Try to be cognizant of it and take care of yourself. Bring as much relaxation into your life as you can.

16. When you are driven to take what feels like drastic measures to keep the peace with your parent, that is often exactly what the situation calls for. The solution you come up with may feel harsh, but it is often better for everyone involved.

17. If your parent is at a nursing home or even a day care facility, you can't be watching them all the time. You cannot be responsible for their offensive behavior. In a way, they can be like little children not knowing that something is wrong to say or do. Make amends when you can.

*Excerpts from Emails to a Friend:*

*I thought a lot about my present situation. Even though I thought this was a really terrible thing when it first happened—for my mom and for me—now I'm thinking maybe it's not. Maybe God is letting me down easy . . . letting me get used to my mom not being there. My mom, the mom that I knew and grew up with up, the mom that nurtured me, and guided me, and counseled me, is basically gone. There is a mom remaining, but she's more like my kid rather than me hers. Did you ever see Invasion of the Body Snatchers—the* original? It's kind of like that. She is there physically, but it's like some of her insides are missing.

These feelings that I'm going through are driving me crazy and killing me. It is so hard to deal with, I can't tell you. I don't know what to feel, I don't know what to think. I don't even know what to hope for. Right now, it really is in the hands of "whatever's meant to be." And I guess I have to leave it at that.

## Chapter 5
## Dementia:  Beam Me Up, Scotty!

### A Little Bit of Dementia

My mother had multi-infarct dementia. Tiny strokes that block blood vessels in the brain and destroy brain tissue cause this condition. Nothing can be done.

Overall, my mother had a low level of dementia, which permitted her to function almost normally. She had no idea that it affected her at all. If you talked to her for just a few minutes, you would probably have no idea that she was affected. But as time wore on, little signs would come forward and it would be clear that she was not all there.

Shortly after her stroke, she exhibited a more pronounced dementia that eventually faded away. Often she spoke of her sister, Bertha, (who had died) who had woken her up, or shared the bed with her, or who wouldn't bring her something that she wanted. Other times she'd ask about her mother and father, and said she didn't remember them dying.

Even during this confusing time, she could still display clarity. I told her that I planned to make myself some pajamas. But I had to alter the pattern which I had never done. When I mentioned that to her, she explained in detail exactly how to do it. Another time she told me about a nurse who rode a motorcycle. She asked me whatever happened with mine. I told her that someone had stolen it. She responded, "Well, they can never register it." A clarity like that amazed me.

Sometimes she would be clear about one thing and confused about something else. Although she spoke to my husband about the price of fish the last time they had gone shopping together, she couldn't remember her roommate's name.

*Depending on the type of dementia and the cause of it, dementia can sometimes come and go. Your parent might be clear on some things and hazy on others. It's all part of the process.*

## Police Academy

Early one evening my mother called to announce there had been a happening. She described how her roommate (who was in an almost permanent fetal position) had stolen her sewing machine. My mother said she either wanted it back or she wanted the one hundred sixty dollars that she had paid for it.

I explained to her the sewing machine was safe in my house. Then she asked if they had gotten the sewing machine out of my house! She wanted me to talk to the police and describe the machine! Nothing I said could convince her that it was in my house. Because she was so convinced that I didn't really have it, she accused me of lying. She said, "I can't trust you anymore. You're not going to get one thing from me until I die and not then either."

On and on she went and wouldn't stop. And she wouldn't listen to reason. I could hear the poor, old woman across from her wailing in the background. My mother ranted on, "Now she's crying and her mother and father are crying and I don't care. (The woman had guests during this incident.) She shouldn't have taken my machine. If she asks nice and knows how to use it, I'll let her. But she shouldn't have taken it without asking. I'll call a policeman and they will come and arrest her."

My mother kept up a constant chatter disparaging the woman and disparaging me. She was freaking out and wouldn't listen to a word I said. Then the phone must have slipped off her ear because she couldn't hear me, and she got angry that I wasn't answering her. She said, "Put your mouth on the receiver like mine. I'm going to have to hang up if you don't talk. Good-by." All I heard was the dial tone.

It wasn't over yet. Ten minutes later, she called back and went through everything again. No matter how many times I told her the machine was at my house, she wouldn't believe me. I finally asked her if she would believe my husband, Dan, and she said yes. He was gentle and patient, but she wouldn't listen to him, either. Then the phone slipped from her ear again and she kept up a constant prattle. My husband said that her voice started to sound weak. Finally, she hung up and didn't call back.

It still wasn't over. The following morning she left a message on my answering machine that said, "I'm anxious to hear what you have to say." I called her, and she still insisted that they had the machine. When I told her the machine was in my house and it had been in my house all along, she said, "Then why did they tell me they had the machine?" It went round and round again with no resolution. I encouraged her to apologize to the woman, and she refused. She wouldn't back down, and she felt certain she was right. When I suggested that it was just a dream or she imagined it, she got angry. She never liked to think that way about herself.

My mother called the police the night this happened. No one knows how she did it. She didn't know the number. Although there was a "911" button on her phone, I had never showed it to her. That doesn't mean that she didn't figure it out for herself. Regardless, she did call them which caused problems. The police called and spoke to a nurse. The nurse explained that it was just an imagined event, and the woman who was supposed to have done the stealing was in the fetal position.

When I called the social worker, our conversation depressed me. She told me that if my mother kept getting worse, then she might have to move to a different facility. The nursing home she was at didn't admit serious dementia-type patients and they couldn't handle her if she continued in that direction. After talking with the nurses, she called me back to say that wouldn't happen for a while and not until they tried everything else first.

My mother had been getting up several times a night and getting dressed thinking it was morning. Her doctor felt that if he gave her an anti-psychotic drug it would not only calm her, but it might make her sleep better.

Next evening she called me again. She started to go on and on about the sewing machine but the phone kept slipping off her ear (like it had done the night before). When she finally got the phone back up to her ear, I told her that it was getting late and I had to go to sleep. I said, "I love you, Mom," and she burst into tears. She said, "I don't deserve this. I'm doing the best that I can." It broke my heart to see her declining like that. I knew that if she got worse it would be a nightmare for everyone, including her.

A week later, they sent my mother to the hospital when they thought she was having another stroke. During the testing, they found that she had a urinary infection. They explained that it could have been the cause for all her aberrant behavior. Urinary tract infections (UTI) often cause confusion. Several days later after the antibiotics had a chance to do their job, her confusion faded and she returned to her semi-normal state.

*If your parent starts behaving wildly, check on any added or subtracted medications. If your parent wears a diaper or sanitary pad for incontinence, arrange a urinary test to check for an infection. It's not always something that is considered.*

## Take Me Home, Country Roads

Another early evening call brought more pain and anguish. My mother wanted me to pick her up at the hotel. I told her she was already home.

Because there was someone there so she couldn't talk loudly, she quietly yelled at me not to tell her that and to just come and take her home. She insisted that she was at a hotel. Trying to be logical in an illogical situation, I asked her to read me the number on the telephone. She told me that it was the hotel's telephone. When I finally got her to read it to me, it was her own telephone in her own room.

I told her that was her telephone number, and it was her bed and her room. She said, "God damn it! Don't tell me that! You give me an answer yes or no!" I asked her where she wanted me to take her. She said that she wanted me to take her to the place she was at when I visited her earlier in the day. I said, "That's where you are right now." Again she started yelling and told me that she was trembling all over. Finally, she said to give her a yes or no. I told her no, that I couldn't come. My mother said, "Okay, so you don't care about me. You don't care that I'm shaking all over." Although I answered, "Yes, I do care about you," she hung up on me before I could finish speaking.

The following morning she called and said she had a bad dream the night before and that I was bad in it. Having a suspicion that this involved the episode on the phone, I asked her to tell me the dream. She said she was in a downtown hotel and there were men there who wanted to sleep with her. Her comment was there was no way she would "do anything" with them. The nurse wanted to get her undressed, but she refused because she didn't want to be with the men. My mother said, "The nurse had to complain to management that I wouldn't let her get me ready. Although the nurse begged and begged, I said I would not lay down for them." Then she continued to tell me that she had called me to take her home and I refused. She said that she had said to herself, "I hate to be mad at her, because she's the only life I have."

When she finished telling me the dream, I told her that not all of it was a dream. I told her how she had called me, yelled at me, and hurt my feelings. Since she didn't respond to what I said, I didn't see any point in carrying it any further.

Later in the conversation, she talked about the elevators there, and I tried to tell her there weren't any. She kept talking about a fourth floor and I told her there wasn't even a second floor. Again she kept arguing and insisting there were elevators. It took a while for me to figure out that she somehow thought the bathroom was the elevator. At least that's what I think she thought.

Another evening, she called and again demanded that I take her home (to the nursing home). When I told her she was home, she yelled at me. "Don't say that again! You know I don't live here!" I tried to explain, but she wouldn't listen at all. She said the place was horrible and there wasn't any bathroom just a toilet beside the bed. She said most of her stuff was there, but it was not her home and she wanted to go home. Then she told me that if I didn't come get her, she would change her will and I wouldn't get a cent. I told her that I loved her, and she said, "I don't think you do." Finally I got her off the phone, but not before she told me she was going to call the police.

The next morning she laughed and said that last night was a dream. None of it happened as far as she was concerned. It felt very weird.

*Occasionally dreams can seem real or real events can get mixed up with a dream. Sometimes it's difficult for a confused aging parent to tell the difference. Sometimes it's hard for the caregiver, as well.*

Dirty Deeds

The first words my mother spoke to me one morning when she called was, "I want to ask you one thing before it's too late. Whose side are you on?" Then she went on to tell me that the night before, her brother and sister had smeared feces all over her. First, she said it was my big brother who had done it. She finally understood that her brother and my brother were different people. But she still kept insisting that her sister and brother had done that terrible thing to her.

When I told her they both lived in Arizona, she insisted they had both been there. She knew her sister was there because she had slept on top of her in bed. Her brother had supposedly eaten with them in the dining room. Finally she said, "Who else could have done this to me? I am utterly unknown."

The day before this happened, she had mentioned to me that she woke up smeared with feces. At that time she intimated that someone else had done it to her, but she didn't say who. What I'm certain happened, is that she had an accident in the middle of the night. Rolling around in bed probably smeared everything all over. Since she only had an accident like that once before right after her stroke, I can see where she might think that someone else had done it.

*Sometimes something that seems real to your parent is borne out of dreams and confusing events. It's best to be understanding, comforting, and loving. It doesn't matter how it happened. It just matters that it upset her.*

Believe It or Not!
A friend of mine told me a story about her aunt who had been in a nursing home before she died. One time she went to visit her and her aunt told her there was a man under her bed. My friend went along with it and asked her aunt if she wanted her to check under the bed for him. Her aunt said, "No, that was last night. He's not there now." My friend just thought her aunt had made up the whole story. Years later after her aunt had died, my friend found out there had been a mental patient in the nursing home who had gone under beds! The story was true!

I had a similar experience with my mother, but I found out the truth much sooner. Another congestive heart episode caused her to be admitted into the hospital. This was another one of those times that after they administered the medications to alleviate her problems, she felt fine almost immediately.

When I went to see her, she acted boisterous and lively. She told me that she had stayed up late the night before teaching the nurses how to play solitaire. She told me that she finally had to ask them to leave, because she felt too tired to play anymore. I "knew" that it had to be a dream, but I didn't see any point in correcting her.

That afternoon when I came back to visit, she was sleeping so I sat on a chair to wait for a while. There were no magazines within reach, and I knew it wouldn't be long before she awoke, so I just sat there and looked around. Surprisingly enough, there on the counter was a deck of large print playing cards! Her story was true!

> Don't be too quick to discount an unbelievable story (like I was!). Sometimes even far-fetched stories can be true. Depending on the situation, it might be better to give your parent the benefit of the doubt.

### Don't Dream a Little Dream of Me

On another one of my mother's many hospital stays, I came to visit. When she saw me she said in a stern voice, "Why did you treat me like that last night?" I told her the last time I saw her was yesterday morning, not night. She said, "You mean you didn't sleep under my bed last night?" I told her that didn't even make sense. After explaining and pleading my case, I think she finally may have believed me.

Another time she called wondering about the mess I made with the company. When I asked her what she was talking about, she said, "Don't ask me questions! You know what company!" When I still said that I didn't know what she was talking about, she began a lengthy dissertation. Her cousins were visiting and when one walked out of the room, the other one disappeared. Since I knew the cousins lived in another state, I asked if she had just woken up and she said she had. I told her

I thought it was just a dream. She said, "You get out of my dream then!"

Even then she wasn't out of the dream yet. She told me she was in a beautiful room in a nice hotel. When I asked her where she was calling from, she told me in the hotel room where she's registered. So I went along with the conversation and told her I would try to find the cousins. Pleased with that, she hung up and never called back.

*Redirect a confused parent if that's possible. If not and if it's safe, go along. Sometimes a parent needs help in getting back to reality. And sometimes it doesn't matter.*

Close But No Banana

One day when I went to visit my mother, she said she was getting ready to go on a three day trip. She wanted to know what day it was, because she was going away Friday, Saturday, and Sunday. There were three neat little piles of clothes—one for each day of the trip. She said that all she needed was a suitcase, but I told her that they would supply it for her. There was no sense in me bringing her a suitcase for an imaginary three day trip.

Several days later, I found out about the three day trip. There had been a field trip planned to go to another town. They were going to leave at ten in the morning and return at three in the afternoon. That's where she had gotten the three from. She often took pieces of things and put them together so they made sense to her and no one else.

Since my mother had a private phone in her room, she often called family and friends, and then would tell me about it on my next visit. One time she told me that she had spoken to her sister, Sally, and that Sally had changed her name to Beverly. I told her it must have been a dream. She got angry and asked why I always think everything is a dream. I told her that at ninety years old it didn't make sense that Sally would suddenly change her name to Beverly. So my mother asked, "Then why did she change her name before?" It was a legitimate question in a backwards sort of way. Sally had changed her name from Sarah very early in her youth. I could see how my mother would think that this was no different.

A week later, I found out the truth about the name change. Her sister, Sally, had moved to a street called Beverly! The story was almost correct—just a little twisted. Again she had the pieces right, but she put them together in the wrong order.

> *Not all truths are as self-evident as others. And often truths can be distorted or twisted. Sometimes what seems to be the truth is just a portion of the truth —which doesn't necessarily mean that it's false—just that it's not as true as it could be.*

## Room to Room

Oftentimes, moving will create confusion in an aging parent who already has cognitive difficulties. Although the nursing home tries to keep moves to a minimum, sometimes it's necessary. Whenever my mother moved from one room to another, it usually caused her problems. Other times she thought she had moved when she hadn't at all.

A couple days after one of her moves, she called me and said she didn't know where anything was. She wanted me to come and explain everything to her. When we hung up and I said I love you, she said, "Not if you don't come and help me."

Another time when I arrived home from work there was a message on my answering machine, "I'm calling from my home wherever that is. Call me if you know where I am." Another message that she left a few days later said, "I wanted to know what date this was. Without you here I have no way of knowing. I know it's Friday, I think. I'll call a little later."

At work on a Monday morning, I found five messages on that answering machine. First, she just left a message. Then she apologized, and then she begged me to answer. Finally, she left a message that she wasn't going to call me anymore. She didn't realize that she was calling me at work instead of at home. I called her immediately and told her that she had left the messages at work, and that I wasn't mad at her. She felt very relieved. I felt bad that I hadn't called her the day before. It's not nice to feel abandoned.

My mother called me one day to say that she was at La Cienega Boulevard. She said, "Do you know where that is?" I said, "Yes, it's by Pico." She said, "Yes, a couple blocks from there." Then she told me that she was in a different place, and that she's different herself. She said this was the first place she's been since she came here.

Sometimes she called to say she was in Omaha, sometimes Iowa, and sometimes Phoenix.

One time she called to tell me that she was in a new place. (She had not moved in some time.) This was a new place, but it was exactly like the old place. The room number was the same and all the same people were there. Almost everything was the same, she said, but it was a different place. This was one of those times there was nothing I could say that would make her right again. I just wanted to hug her and ease her pain and confusion.

> *Confusion is sad for both you and your parent. Comfort them, explain to them when you can, but always be sensitive to their needs.*

## Doctors, Strangers, and Friends

Whenever my mother had a doctor's appointment, she became focused on it to the exclusion of everything else. A few days before her doctor's appointment she called me at midnight to find out if the appointment was that morning. When I told her it was midnight, she said, "Oh no! I just got dressed and all painted up!" She said she was sorry and hung up.

A couple days later, she called at five in the morning to see when her doctor's appointment was. Again I told her that she was a little early and it wasn't for another day. On the day of her appointment, she called again. I tried to explain that her appointment wasn't for three hours. She had no idea what I was talking about. She felt so excited and so agitated about the entire ordeal that she couldn't think straight. After the appointment was over she was equally spacey, because she felt so exhausted from the anticipation and the event itself.

When my mother had an evaluation by a gerontology psychological team, she felt exhausted for two days afterward. Two hours of intense excitement and stimulation were more than she could handle. Sometimes it would appear that she had had another stroke, when it was just sheer exhaustion. She would get that way sometimes if someone special, who didn't come to visit often, visited her.

> Often excitement or exhaustion can cause some short-term dementia in an aging parent. After they have become used to a sedentary lifestyle, anything out of the ordinary can tax them. That's not to say it's a bad thing. Change in daily routine can add an enjoyable diversion to an elder's life. My mother received much enjoyment from the very events that caused her difficulties.

## Bits and Pieces of Dementia

Something that plagued me off and on during my mother's stay at the nursing home was her telephone. While she'd talk to me on the phone, she would inadvertently let the phone slip down so she couldn't hear me anymore. It was frustrating for me, and probably equally frustrating for her. I would have to yell at her as loud as I could for her to put the phone on her ear. Sometimes she'd insist that it was already there, and yet she still couldn't hear me. Finally, I got the idea for her to switch ears when that happened, and that usually fixed the problem. If she could hear me tell her to switch ears! Once when I visited her, she received a phone call and I could see the other side of the situation. As she talked the phone slowly slid down her cheek until the earpiece was at her chin and the mouthpiece on her chest. She still kept talking as fast as she could think of things to say. With no idea the phone had slipped down, she didn't realize there was even a problem.

Not realizing something is happening or not happening is definitely a part of dementia. My mother told me one day on the phone that she had been sleepwalking naked. She said that she just had on a blouse, one stocking, and no pants and she went to the dining room to eat breakfast. On and on she went about sleepwalking, but it happened at seven in the morning. Months later while my mother used the restroom, a nurse told me what had happened the night before. About midnight my mother had woken up and then climbed into someone else's bed—with them. The following morning she was still confused. She was in the bathroom half naked, and when the nurse wanted to help her finish getting dressed, she insisted that she was already dressed. It took some quick talking to convince her to dress appropriately for breakfast.

My mother was adamant about mice stealing her chocolate cookies that I had brought for her. We lived in the country and had mice a time or two, and I knew what the signs were. Mice always left "calling cards" wherever they went. I checked everywhere around the cookies and everywhere else and never found any evidence of mice. Still, she was convinced that they had stolen her cookies. She only wanted me to bring her two cookies at a time, so she could eat them right then. Nothing I could say would dissuade her from the non-existent mice.

Telling time probably isn't something you would think to find in the dementia category. Although my mother had a digital clock for twenty years by her bedside, after her stroke she could not tell time with a digital clock. I had bought her one never considering that it might be a problem. The following day she called me, and I spent fifteen minutes attempting to explain how to tell time with it. She just didn't get it, and she wanted me to take it back and get her another clock.

Shortly after my mother moved into a different section of the nursing home, she tried to talk her old roommate into sharing a room together again. Since she had browbeaten the poor woman during their time together, the woman politely refused. My mother, embarrassed and angry, struck back at the woman by saying, "I'm prettier than you!" A comment a child might make when she didn't get her way.

My mother often struggled for words and had a hard time putting sentences together. Although she played bingo every week without fail, sometimes she couldn't remember the word bingo. Sometimes when she had difficulty finding words, she would substitute a word that made no sense, like "fashion" or "nugget" which had nothing to do with the sentence. Other times, she would make up her own word. She couldn't remember the word for buttons, so she called them, "pinkles." Other times she would shock me with her vocabulary. One evening as we talked on the phone someone came into her room, so she told me she would call me back, but she didn't. The next day I asked her why she never called me back. First, she asked if she was supposed to. When I explained to her what had happened, she said, "Oh well, it was of no consequence anyway!"

I laughed and she started giggling. She said, "I got that word out! I could have used some smaller words, but that one cost less!" She just kept giggling.

*Mild dementia can display itself in many ways, some more surprising than others. Be as understanding and gentle as possible. If you can laugh the pain away, that's great. If you can get your parent to laugh, that's even better.*

## Sense and Sensibilities

Just as a small child is apt to do or say anything, our aging parents who have even the first touches of dementia are sometimes lacking in good judgment. These lapses of good judgment can be as simple as doing or saying something impolite, to not being able to judge distances or amounts, or doing something contrary to the person they once were. My mother's lapses of good judgment usually pertained to the latter two.

Once a week, my mother received a whirlpool bath which she loved. She'd play in the bubbles and enjoy herself thoroughly, while the nurse on duty washed her hair and helped her wash herself. The rest of the week, my mother gave herself a sponge bath. While the basin filled with water, she would put in some liquid soap. Not realizing when the bottle neared empty, she wouldn't tell me she needed soap until it was gone. It seemed like we were constantly buying bottles of liquid soap, so my husband got the brilliant idea of buying her a big bottle, so we wouldn't have to worry about it for a while. Wrong. The big bottle was empty almost sooner than the smaller bottles. She just could not judge how much soap to put in the basin of water. Not to mention that she couldn't determine when it was "almost" empty so she could ask me in advance.

One memorable Thanksgiving, my husband and I arrived to share in her annual Thanksgiving dinner. She was in the bathroom when we arrived, because she had just had an "accident." While she cleaned herself, I went to get her another diaper-panty liner. I saw that her blouse was soiled, so I told her to take it off. She held up a fecal stained corner and said, "I rubbed it all off. It's fine. I'm wearing it." The smell in the bathroom was horrific. There was no way I was spending my Thanksgiving sitting next to someone who smelled like that, whether she was my mother or not. I insisted that she take it off. Luckily, I had brought her a new outfit out of storage; otherwise I may not have been able to convince her to change her clothes. As it was, she wanted to wear her pants that she claimed were still clean. When I picked them up, I noticed a small piece of fecal matter clinging to the waistband. I cleaned it off and threw it into her dirty clothes pile. My mother, who at ninety-four years old still wore make-up every day and still prided herself on her clothes, was willing to wear something that had fecal matter smeared all over it. To Thanksgiving dinner no less! Sometimes the changes that had befallen her were too much to bear. The rest of the time they were just overwhelming.

As time passes and your parent's once good judgment dissolves into just a memory, be patient and kind. The changes that you see in your parent are often invisible to them. They don't know that their judgment is not as sound as it used to be, and so they don't realize it should be questioned.

* * * * *

Points to Remember:

1. Depending on the type of dementia and the cause of it, dementia can sometimes come and go. Your parent might be clear on some things and hazy on others. It's all part of the process.
2. If your parent starts behaving wildly, check on any added or subtracted medications. If your parent wears a diaper or sanitary pad for incontinence, arrange a urinary test to check for an infection. It's not always something that is considered.
3. Occasionally dreams can seem real or real events can get mixed up with a dream. Sometimes it's difficult for a confused aging parent to tell the difference. Sometimes it's hard for the caregiver, as well.
4. Sometimes something that seems real to your parent is borne out of dreams and confusing events. It's best to be understanding, comforting, and loving. It doesn't really matter how it happened. It just matters that it upset her.
5. Don't be too quick to discount an unbelievable story (like I was!). Sometimes even far-fetched stories can be true. Depending on the situation, it might be better to give your parent the benefit of the doubt.
6. Redirect a confused parent if that's possible. If not, and if it's safe, go along. Sometimes a parent needs help in getting back to reality. And sometimes it doesn't matter.

7. Not all truths are as self-evident as others. And often truths can be distorted or twisted. Sometimes what seems to be the truth is just a portion of the truth—which doesn't necessarily mean that it's false—just that it's not as true as it could be.

8. Confusion is sad for both you and your parent. Comfort them, explain to them when you can, but always be sensitive to their needs.

9. Often excitement or exhaustion can cause some short-term dementia in an aging parent. After they have become used to a sedentary lifestyle, anything out of the ordinary can tax them. That's not to say it's a bad thing. Change in daily routine can add an enjoyable diversion to an elder's life.

10. Mild dementia can display itself in many ways, some more surprising than others. Be as understanding and gentle as possible. If you can laugh the pain away, that's great. If you can get your parent to laugh, that's even better.

11. As time passes and your parent's once good judgment dissolves into just a memory, be patient and kind. The changes that you see in your parent are often invisible to them. They don't know that their judgment is not as sound as it used to be, and so they don't realize it should be questioned.

## Advice from My Brother:

*Re the Original vs. the Now Mom, and your reaction to what's happening: I see it as a matter of context. You are taking all this stuff seriously, as if her outrageous behavior is normal or not normal. It is neither. She is nuts, demented, hallucinating, tripping, chemically altered and just plain crazy. If she were in a mental hospital, would you be upset* by this kind of behavior? No, you would say, Well, Mom's in the Nuthouse and this is how they behave here.

So just try seeing her as being in the Nursing Home for the Mentally Impaired. Hey, she's acting like a nutcase because she IS a nutcase!!. The strokes have scrambled her brains and what you are experiencing is not so off the wall.

Back off. Just watch her from a distance. Don't get involved. Agree with what she says, and just nod your head. Don't see her so often. Let the nursing home staff deal with her. That is their job. They are used to dealing with people who have had strokes and whose brains are scrambled.

## Chapter 6
## Health Issues: Sticks and Stones Can Break My Bones

<u>Red Is the Color</u>
    About a year and a half before my mother had her stroke, she had some rectal bleeding. Back then, she was hospitalized and they performed a colonoscopy and some other tests. They diagnosed her problem as diverticulosis. Her doctor told us the bleeding would hopefully stop by itself, but if not, then she would have to undergo surgery. Eventually, the bleeding did stop by itself, and she had no more problems with it.
    After she was in the nursing home, and almost a year to the day of her previous bleeding problem, I received a call from a nurse that she had been bleeding. I remembered her hospitalization from before and how scary it all was; and I felt bad that my mother had to go through it all again.
    Since there was just the one major bleeding incident, her doctor ordered blood work to monitor her blood loss but he didn't hospitalize her. Unfortunately, because of the potential for more blood loss, he had to take her off the blood thinning medication that helped prevent further strokes. Oftentimes, treating the elderly consists of balancing medications and ailments.

My poor mother felt awful about the incident. When it happened, the blood mixed with feces came rushing out of her. There was nothing she could do, and it made a terrible mess. She kept apologizing to the nurses for the extra work. Besides a small stomachache and feeling weak, she was okay. She had come through another potentially deadly situation.

*Health issues that have been a problem in the past might recur. Keep abreast of all health problems.*

## The Dating Game

Not long after the bleeding incident, I received another call one morning. The nurse said that my mother had fallen during the night and had possibly broken her wrist. I arranged to meet my mother at the emergency room. The x-rays showed that she had broken her wrist. They put a splint on her arm so she wouldn't do any more damage and sent her home. That afternoon, I met her at the orthopedic doctor's office. After examining her wrist and looking at the x-rays, he arranged the surgery for that evening. Back at the hospital, I waited with her until it was time for the surgery. She wasn't afraid. She just wanted to get it over with.

The surgery went smoothly, and an hour later my mother rested in the recovery room. When they finally allowed me in there, I found her fully awake and entertaining the nurses with her quick wit. She had everyone laughing and enjoying her company. The surgeon had written on her chart, "very sociable." I got a kick out of that. Although she was in good spirits, it had been a long night and a long day for her and she was ready to go to sleep. A nurse picked her up from the hospital and brought her back to the nursing home where she rested comfortably through the night.

The following morning I received a call that they thought the cast was too tight. Because the doctor who had done the surgery was off, they took my mother to the emergency room to have it checked. In my youth, I worked for a veterinarian and once when an animal's leg swelled and the person didn't call to get it corrected, the animal lost its leg. So, the possibly too-tight cast concerned me. I met my mother at the emergency room. When the doctor examined her, he didn't think the cast was too tight. Since he wasn't an orthopedic doctor, it still worried me. He told her to keep the arm elevated and sent her home. When I called her later that day, she complained the cast still bothered her.

The next day the doctor who did the surgery was called. He said to take her back to the emergency room and have them split the cast to make it looser. After that, I felt better about the whole situation. Since the cast wasn't as uncomfortable for my mother, I could rest much easier. Several weeks later, the doctor removed the cast and everything was fine. Although the wrist wasn't as flexible as before, at least there was no pain in it.

The humorous part of this not-so-humorous story is how she came to break her wrist. In the middle of the night, she had a dream about having a hot date. My mother, who always has to look just so, wanted to wash up and put on her make-up. Somewhere between her bed and the mirror, she fell down. She said her wrist started hurting right away, but she thought she was still in the dream. She told the pain to go away because it was just a dream. Just then a nurse came in and rescued her.

*If your parent has a broken bone or other health problem, stay vigilant and make sure that everything gets taken care of properly.*

<u>Heimlich Who?</u>
My mother always loved watermelon. During the summer, I'd bring her a container full of small bite-sized pieces of watermelon. Every time I brought it, she appreciated it and enjoyed it tremendously.

One afternoon I sat watching as she ate her watermelon. She talked a mile a minute and kept eating as fast as she could. Suddenly, she had one of her coughing spells. Since they were chronic and she had them all the time, I didn't pay much attention. But this time she must have inhaled a piece of watermelon. I looked over as she struggled to breathe. I jumped up, stepped behind her, and performed the Heimlich Maneuver. Or at least what I thought it should to be! I'd never done it before and it was a little difficult with my mother in a wheelchair. But the watermelon popped out, and five minutes later she was talking and eating watermelon again as if nothing had happened.

Before I left, I told her that I wanted to take the rest of the watermelon home with me, because I felt afraid that I had cut the pieces too big. She didn't want me to. I said, "How would I feel if you choked again and died?" She said, "If you did it on purpose, that's one thing. But if you didn't do it on purpose, then it's not your fault, and it was just my time to go." My mother was still as flippant about death as she had always been.

*Always be prepared for anything! You never know what surprises may await you with an aging parent.*

A Shot in the Dark
　　　Sometimes as your parent approaches the end of the journey, you may need to make decisions that you don't want to make or are difficult to make. For me, flu shots were one of those decisions. First, I received a call from a nurse asking if I wanted my mother to have a pneumonia shot. My immediate response was to deflect the question and tell the nurse to do whatever my mother's doctor wanted. After giving it some thought, I called back and told her no, I did not want my mother to have a pneumonia shot.
　　　Then the nurse called back asking if my mother should have a flu shot. I told her that I'd have to think about it and call her back. You would think the "no extraordinary measures" paperwork would cover this, but it doesn't. It's a decision you may have to make every year.
　　　When I put everything together, I finally decided that I didn't think the original mom would have want a flu shot. She never wanted to be in this "condition," she had not been feeling well around the time this came up, and she had deteriorated mentally. This was not something the original mom would have wanted to continue indefinitely. She did not have a flu shot the year before and she made it through fine. My mother was incredibly tough and I felt that if she was meant to get through it, she would. I didn't think

at this point in her life that I should be taking actions to keep her alive longer than nature intended. It's just not what she would have wanted.

*Having to decide whether your parent should have a flu shot or other preventives will come up. Give it some thought and decide what is right for both of you.*

<u>Rosebud</u>
During the many months that my mother spent at the nursing home, she had more than six episodes of congestive heart failure/heart attacks (sometimes both around the same time). She also had more than fifteen mini-strokes or transient ischemic attacks (TIA) that we knew of or guessed at. Sometimes she just didn't act right, other times you knew something was going on but it wasn't clear what it was. In addition, she had fallen or slid to the floor numerous times.

One day when I came to visit, I found my mother parked outside the hair salon waiting to have her nails done. She was sleeping when I arrived and I woke her up. She couldn't talk. All she could do was say, "one." She'd even try to spell it, one slow letter at a time. Over and over again she repeated "one" until the manicurist finished her nails. Then she somehow indicated that she wanted to go to sleep. She wanted me to call a nurse to help her lay down because she couldn't do it herself. This was unlike my mother who always insisted on doing everything by herself. I knew she was having some kind of stroke episode and I thought that her repeating "one" was some profound philosophical breakthrough or something. It turned out that she only wanted one coat of nail polish on her nails!

There was another series of mini-stroke episodes that added up to the week from hell. When I went to see my mother she was sleeping. I woke her but she couldn't stay awake. When she could find the words to talk, she slurred the words and mixed them up. She said she had a headache and didn't want to eat lunch. Before I left, she said that I could go and that she would just lie there and suffer.

I immediately went to talk to the charge nurse who checked her out and said she'd keep an eye on her. Even with extra attention, I still worried about her. Later that evening I called and found out she was normal again. She said she thought she was going to die, and she was angry that I had left her there alone. I told her that I had gone to the head nurse who called me with her progress.

Two days later when I spoke to my mother in the morning, she said she had another "spell" the night before and still wasn't feeling good. When I came in to see her, she was sleeping again. After waking, she felt weak and kept falling back to sleep. Before I left she said to me, "You don't have to worry about me. I'll either get better or die."

That afternoon when I went to see her, she felt a little better. When I went to see her the following day, she was active, happy, and feeling good. But she did say that she thought that was "it" and she said, "At ninety-three, what can you expect?"

Those few days scrambled my emotions. When she felt poorly, I tried to psych myself for letting her go, and the next I knew she felt fine again. Then I felt good about her being okay, and she turned around and looked like she was going to die. Every time I talked to her or went to see her, there was either drastic improvement or drastic decline. The back and forth and in-between were killing me. I wasn't sure if I would survive my mother's death.

The following day when I went in, she was the weakest she had been. She could barely talk, couldn't find the words, and couldn't manage to pick up her head. I spent our time together rubbing her arm and trying to comfort her during what I thought were her final moments. Two days later, she was fine and back to her cantankerous self. My mother, indomitable spirit that she was, again conquered her health problems and lived over a year longer.

*Sometimes small health problems add up. Each transient ischemic attack my mother had did a little more damage to her brain. Each heart attack she had did a little more damage to her heart. All you can do is be supportive and give comfort when it's needed.*

### A Pain in the Butt

One afternoon shortly after the multiple stroke week, I went in to visit my mother. When she saw me she burst into tears. She told me that she had diarrhea and that her butt was red and sore. I asked if she wanted some cream or lotion put on to soothe the soreness, and she said the nurses had already done that but it still hurt.

My mother wanted to call my brother, so I dialed the number for her. She said to him, "How's your life going? I hope it's going better than mine." After telling him about her strokes and her butt problems she said, ". . . so give me a little pity."

The following day when I spoke to her on the phone, she cried again about her butt problem. Because she sounded so terrible, I felt compelled to go see her. When I arrived, she lay crosswise on the bed with her feet and legs hanging over the edge. She asked me to move her legs onto the bed for her. When I did that, she still couldn't shift the rest of her body by herself. My mother had always been so defensive over her independence. It was difficult to see her lying there so helpless and vulnerable like a baby. In a couple days, the diarrhea had cleared up along with the sore butt and she was back to her old self again. Another crisis had passed.

Just as diarrhea can be serious for a baby in diapers, it can be serious for an aging parent in diapers or helper pads. Make sure it gets taken care of properly so more serious problems do not develop.

Piece by Piece
After my mother recovered sufficiently from her first and most damaging stroke, she realized she couldn't see very well. She was told that sometimes it takes a while after a stroke for the eyes to adjust or get back to where they were. My mother was always an avid reader, and this took a huge part of her life away. She lost all interest in books. I offered to bring her books on tape, but she showed no interest. It hurt me that she had lost such an important part of her life.

Her eyes never did improve and I think they gradually got worse. She would often think she saw things that were not really there. One afternoon she pointed out a mouse on the windowsill. It was the knob to open the window. Another time, she showed me a beetle on the floor that she had killed. It was a slight blemish in the linoleum. She always had a great imagination, and her imperfect vision helped that imagination along.

Lydia, the Activities Director, told me that sometimes my mother confused her and another woman with similar hair coloring and style. Another time, Lydia introduced her to a ten-year-old volunteer with bright red hair. My mother thought it was me (although my hair isn't red). When Lydia corrected her, she said the ten-year-old girl and I had the same shape. I suppose that her eyes were so bad that shape was the only way she could identify someone.

On another visit to my mother, I showed her something and she said she couldn't see it because it was so dark in the room. The shades were open and the room was bright. I said something about her eyes and she said it had been pretty dark lately. I asked her if maybe it was another stroke coming, and she said, "No, it's just been like that." All I could do was hug her for her loss.

Lydia told me about another time when they were participating in some activity that involved using their hands. She said that my mother had a hard time with it, but she eventually accomplished what she wanted and was really into it. One time I brought in a needle and thread for her to experiment with. She wanted to sew her own clothes again (like she had done all her life), and I told her that I didn't think she could. We finally agreed that if she could sew on a button, then I

would agree. As I watched her struggle to do what had come so easy for her for so many years, it tore me up. I had to bite my lip and squinch my eyes together to keep tears from rolling down my face.
I thought I had proven my point, but my mother, undaunted, still insisted she could do it.

    Although my mother used the wheelchair for her primary locomotion, she was not "confined to a wheelchair." Twice a day, she exercised by using her "four-wheeler," which is how she referred to her walker. She enjoyed using it and all the attention she got as she walked up and down the hallways. At some point, she must have had another mini-stroke that only damaged her left foot. Suddenly it started dragging, and she could no longer walk with her walker. That upset her very much. I think the walker gave her a certain amount of freedom that most of the other residents didn't have. She liked that it set her apart from the rest. The physical therapy department made her a brace to use that helped, but it wasn't the same and she wasn't as comfortable doing her walking. Eventually, she was able to use the walker again without the brace, but she didn't have as much confidence in her abilities as before.

    Her body was falling apart piece by piece. First her eyes, then her hands, and then her feet. It felt like she was slipping away from me one piece at a time.

> *Your aging parent is getting older every minute. Although everyone is, toward the end of the journey the deterioration seems to accelerate.*

## The Big C

There was an ethereal otherworldly quality outside the day I found out that my mother had lung cancer. Mist surrounded everything. It seemed an appropriate match to how I felt. The news devastated me. I wondered what the world that she was going to was like. I wondered what my world would be like without her. The news didn't seem real—almost like it was happening to someone else.

It started just like a "normal" crisis. A nurse called me at six in the morning saying that my mother was having a hard time breathing and needed to go to the hospital. When I got to the hospital, they had already given her the drug to help eliminate the extra fluid in her lungs. She still struggled for breath. Her blood pressure started high in the extreme danger range. As she eliminated some of the fluid, it started dropping to the too low range. Her heart was tired and it looked like this might be the end.

While holding her hand and patting her arm, I tried to comfort her. I told her to relax and let go. I didn't want to hold her back if she was ready to die and I didn't want to hurry her along if she still wanted to live. Then her blood pressure starting rising to normal. She was coming back.

They admitted her into the hospital and she immediately fell asleep. When she woke up at ten o'clock, she ate a huge breakfast and said that she felt like she had never been sick. She told me that she thought this was her last day but she wasn't afraid. She just wondered what would happen to the cookies that I had brought her the day before!

When I spoke to her doctor, he said he was encouraged about her heart problems because of how fast she sprang back, but he had seen a shadow on her chest x-ray. He wanted to consult with the radiologist. When he called me back, he said the radiologist did think it was lung cancer. A CT scan confirmed the diagnosis.

It's strange that when I thought my mother was going to die from a heart problem, it didn't bother me nearly as much as when I found out she had lung cancer. There is something deadly and evil about cancer. It has an insidious quality that makes even strong people shudder at the thought. To die from a heart attack seemed so much more gentle and merciful than the slow and prolonged suffering from cancer.

Her doctor said that her lung cancer was not aggressive and there was a good chance that her heart would kill her before the lung cancer affected her. Two months later when she had another congestive heart episode and another chest x-ray, it confirmed that. The cancer had not grown at all in two months. We never told my mother, and she never exhibited any obvious symptoms.

*Sometimes unexpected events will happen. One crisis will turn into another. What's most important is comforting your parent and making them feel loved.*

## What About Me?!

My health started suffering as soon as my mom had her stroke. All the extra jobs to do, the extra time required, worrying about her and caring for her all added up to a bundle of stress. And all that stress had to come out somehow. It came out in chest pains and severe headaches.

I was no stranger to headaches. My job and past circumstances with my mom had brought them on previously. The headaches themselves, brought on by stress, caused me more stress because it was something else for me to worry about. A neighbor was kind enough to offer to come visit me in the hospital after I had a stroke of my own! The reality of that comment hit me hard. But I felt too overwhelmed to do anything about it.

A close friend who had already been through the whole caregiving routine with her mother scared me. In the middle of her stressful situation, she got breast cancer. The doctor told her the stress had definitely been a factor. That wasn't the only warning I had.

In the books I read on caregiving, there was either the caregiver getting cancer or the spouse getting some new and critical disease. In television shows featuring caregiving themes it was the same story. Either the caregivers themselves or their spouses were affected. Usually when the spouse got something, it was an instant critical condition, like an aggressive cancer or hospitalization for an unknown but serious malady.

After reading so much about this and wondering if it would happen to me and my husband, I began to call this the "what about me?" condition. This applies especially with the spouse. When the caregiver devotes most of his or her time to the aging parent, the spouse needs more attention. "What about me?" I do not mean to belittle the situation at all. Certainly these spouses did not purposely bring the dreadful diseases on themselves. And even with the caregiver, the "what about me?" is their own body crying out that it needs some attention. Too many caregivers forget about their own needs and their family's needs—not deliberately, but because caregiving consumes their life.

A friend in a similar caregiving position as me, confided that her husband began having seizures shortly after she moved her feeble and ailing mother up from another state. This friend also works two jobs to support the extra expense of her mother. How long will it be before her body cries out, "What about me?"

My own chest pains and headaches dwindled down when the issues surrounding my mother's stroke began to settle. Of course, there always seemed to be one crisis or another which brought on a new onslaught of pain. Since I didn't have the time or resources for a weekly massage, I tried to find my own ways to relax. I meditated when I could, tried breathing deeply often, walked out in nature to appreciate the beauty of a flower or the song of a bird—anything to get my thoughts away from what caused me stress. So far, my husband and I are both healthy. I can only hope that being aware of a potential problem and trying to stop it is enough to prevent it from happening.

*Be aware of your own needs and your family's needs during your caregiving experience. Your health and well-being are important. Don't let guilt force you to neglect other important areas of your life.*

\* \* \* \* \*

Points to Remember:

1. Health issues that have been a problem in the past might recur. Keep abreast of all health problems.

2. If your parent has a broken bone or other health problem, stay vigilant and make sure that everything gets taken care of properly.

3. Always be prepared for anything! You never know what surprises may await you with an aging parent.

4. Having to decide whether your parent should have a flu shot or other preventives will come up. Give it some thought and decide what is right for both of you.

5. Sometimes small health problems add up. All you can do is be supportive and give comfort when it's needed.

6. Just as diarrhea can be serious for a baby in diapers, it can be serious for an aging parent in diapers or helper pads. Make sure it gets taken care of properly so more serious problems do not develop.

7. Your aging parent is getting older every minute. Although everyone is, toward the end of the journey the deterioration seems to accelerate.

8. Sometimes unexpected events will happen. One crisis will turn into another. What's most important is comforting your parent and making them feel loved.

9. Be aware of your own needs and your family's needs during your caregiving experience. Your health and well-being are important. Don't let guilt force you to neglect other important areas of your life.

*Email Excerpt After One of Many Health Episodes:*
*She's doing great now, and wheeling all over the place, talking to everyone and showing off her clothes. The social worker today told her that she gets the best dressed at the nursing home award, and of course she was thrilled to hear that. Some things never change!*

## Chapter 7
## Sex, Drugs, and Rock 'n' Roll

### Sex

My mother dreaming about having a hot date was just the tail of the comet compared to her other sexual dreams and fantasies. Sometimes it seemed like sex was all she talked about. Apparently, this is not uncommon in the elderly!

One evening she called and told me there were all these "rough men" around. She said she was afraid to go to sleep with them around because she didn't want them to have their way with her.

My mother had several dreams that she told me about where she was in the basement (there was no basement where she lived) and there were men and women down there pairing off and having sex. She always said that she never wanted any part of that. In one particularly painful dream, all the women had lined up against the wall waiting for a man to choose them. My mother said she stood there naked with the rest of the women. One by one the women were chosen, and no one chose her! A terrible dream that was both scary and humiliating. It was one step worse than not being chosen for basketball.

It wasn't enough that my mother had dreams and fantasies about sex, she had to involve other people. Once she told me about a friend of hers, Brenda, that "really wants a man." I asked her how she knew that, and she responded, "I can feel it!" She also said that she didn't want a man because she was too old for them. Since she wouldn't even consider any of the old men who lived there, she was talking about the male nurses and other male employees. A couple months later, speaking again of Brenda, she said that Brenda was supposed to get married, but the guy must have found out what kind of person she was and called it off. She told me that she and Brenda were at a bar one time, and that Brenda went off with some guy that she didn't know and had sex with him. If you think there is a hint of truth to any of these stories, there is no bar or anything that could be mistaken for a bar at the nursing home. And I can guarantee that going to a bar was NOT on the list of field trips!

Her next wild imagining concerned a short term roommate that she had, Evelyn. This poor woman was in the fetal position, could barely get out of bed even with help, and was close to death. My mother went on and on about how Evelyn and a male nurse had "a party" the night before. Her proof was they had washed up together "afterwards." Perhaps a cigarette afterwards would have been more convincing. My mother said that she had gone over it and over it in her head, and she is certain that it happened. I explained to her the woman is on her deathbed and I didn't think that she could screw (I actually used the "f" word here) anyone. Her response was that maybe Evelyn wanted one last screw (she used the "f" word here) before she died. That cracked me up, but I still didn't believe her story. She was convinced though.

Another time she told me that she had spent the night with my father (who has been dead for more than forty years). I asked if they had sex, and she said no, they just slept together. And yet another time she told me that she had gotten married and her husband had just left. Later she told me that was a mistake, that she really wasn't married. She's often made comments about men, speaking of them as "her boyfriend" and such, and then she says that she still wouldn't "do it" with him.

The best example of my mother's blatant sexuality came the morning after she was hospitalized for congestive heart failure. She confided to me the night before she had dreamed she had married a male employee at the nursing home who would often recite poetry to her. At first, she didn't want to have sex with him and then she thought, "What the heck!" Then she went on to say they were having sex and she couldn't come. That is the exact word my mother used! It's hard to imagine your elderly parent using that term! Continuing, she said that she tried and tried and finally did. She explained that that's when she woke up having a hard time breathing. Then she told me the last time she had congestive heart failure, she also had a dream like that! Great. Every time my mother has a wet dream, she gets congestive heart failure!

Again, these thoughts, fantasies, and dreams about sex are not unusual in the elderly. A friend told me that her elderly aunt accused my friend's mother of having sex with a group of men in a nearby park. The aunt even warned her brother what a slut his wife was!

*Remember that your parent is an adult and has "been there and done that." These feelings are normal and you should not ridicule your parent or make him or her feel ashamed.*

Drugs

It is my understanding that Medicare pays for a certain amount of drugs, but there are still some big and possibly expensive loopholes. In addition, the monthly cost of the nursing home does not include drugs. Drugs cost extra! And they are expensive.

For months after my mother entered the nursing home I struggled with making copies of her drug bills and sending them to her supplemental insurance company. After I'd receive their checks, I'd have to compare what they paid to what they should have paid. Nearly a year later when I was on the phone with the pharmacy the nursing home went through, I found out there was an easier way. I didn't have to send copies! I didn't have to compare! And most importantly, my mother's insurance company had an agreement with the pharmacy, who discounted all her medications!

Once I discovered this wonderful information, all the work was carried out without any effort from me. I would pay the pharmacy each month when their bill came, and the insurance company would automatically send their reimbursement. No more making copies, struggling with the amounts, and comparing two amounts that didn't match. It was all taken care of for me, and handled much more efficiently than when I did it.

There is another important point to consider regarding aging parents, whether they are in or out of nursing homes. Most aging parents take medications for blood pressure, cholesterol, or something. And most of them take multiple medications. Oftentimes, these medications create a change that is unintended: they cause cognitive problems. Too often drugs are the unsuspected culprit when cognitive difficulties become apparent. If your parent has a sudden onset of confusion or forgetfulness, always keep the drug interaction possibility in mind.

Some medications like sleeping pills, sedatives, or tranquilizers are the more obvious possibilities. It is the least obvious medications that cause the most problems, because no one suspects them. Some glaucoma eye drops, some incontinence medications, and even some blood pressure drugs can cause cognitive difficulties.

A friend said her mother had suddenly acted confused and they thought she couldn't continue living alone like she wanted. Her mother called her one day and asked where she was. My friend said, "You're home." Her mother did not have any idea. When my friend reported this incident to her mother's doctor and asked about new drugs she might be taking, he took her off her new arthritis medicine and the confusion left almost immediately.

*Contact the pharmacy to see if they have an agreement with your parent's insurance company (most do). If you notice new cognitive difficulties, find out immediately if your parent has taken any new medications.*

Rock 'n' Roll

An important but often forgotten aspect of caring for an aging parent is entertainment. If your parent's eyes are still fine and they enjoy watching television and/or reading like my mother did before her stroke, then your task will be easier. But if your parent's eyes are too weak for that, then some form of daily entertainment is necessary. If they are at home, adult day care is a possibility. From what I understand, adult day care has great elder activities, and aging parents will usually enjoy it if given the chance.

Make sure any nursing home you choose has a good activities program. This is as important as the quality of the daily care. The nursing home my mother lived in was lucky to have an activities director who was not only creative with the activities, but she could have been an entertainer as well. She put her heart into the activities and made sure they were fun. Just being around her bubbly personality made you feel good. During any activity, you could always expect a few laughs as well. Some nursing homes aren't places to die, but places to have fun.

The favorite activity at the nursing home was bingo. Shortly after my mother arrived there, I came to visit and noticed that she had on a new pair of earrings. I asked her where she got them and she said bingo! Another time when I called her, she was involved in a sing-a-long of some sort. The activities help some aging parents adjust to nursing home life. Others, like my mother's last roommate, Ginny, needed some encouragement to go to the activities, but once there thoroughly enjoyed them. It all depends on your parent's personality. My mother was always social and liked being around people. That's why for her, nursing home life was much preferable to being home alone with one nurse for company.

There are many other activities to choose from like piano music and singing, crafts, stories read aloud, movies, music videos, karaoke, religious services on Sundays, and residents' birthday parties. The nursing home also plans special events like children from a school coming in to sing and give out handmade gifts for each of the residents. They also had a beauty/barber shop for those interested and someone going around with Avon or Mary Kay. My mother loved having her nails done at the beauty shop and was always the first in line for the cosmetics.

Holidays are another special time in a nursing home. Decorations, traditional food, and parties help to make the days stand out from the rest. Some holidays feature family dinners shared with the residents. My mother enjoyed those times the most. She would dress up and have something to look forward to.

Another item not often considered but definitely fitting into the entertainment category is the telephone. My mother received much enjoyment by calling her friends and family. With a private line, they could call her without having to wait for the community phone to be connected. It was a lifeline out to the world.

Of course, there were those times that I cursed myself for giving her a phone. Like those many calls in the middle of the night when she would ask when I'm coming to visit or ask what time it was when it was midnight. For a while, these calls occurred regularly and were annoying. Then they tapered off with only an occasional lapse. The mistake I almost made before I came to my senses was to program her phone so she could reach me with just a press of one button. She obviously had no trouble punching up our number. Programming her phone would have only served to make accidental calls more prevalent and more disturbing.

If you decide to get a phone for your parent, be sure that when you call the phone company to set it up, you make yourself the main contact and put a block on switching long distance carriers. I didn't do that, and it almost turned out to be a nightmare. Unbeknownst to me, my mother changed long distance carriers, which in and of itself was no big deal. But, she often made international calls and her new long distance service didn't include that. Luckily, I caught the potential problem before she made any calls. When I found out, I was angry with them having switched without my knowledge. But on the phone, if you caught my mother just right, you would have no idea that she was old and semi-feeble minded. So, I couldn't blame them. I did, however, immediately block any more changes to the long distance carrier!

Entertainment is a critical part of your parent's journey. Make sure they have plenty to keep them busy. This will keep them happy and you happier.

* * * * *

## Points to Remember:

1. Remember that your parent is an adult and has "been there and done that." These feelings are normal and your parent should not be ridiculed or made to feel ashamed.
2. Contact the pharmacy to see if they have an agreement with your parent's insurance company (most do). If you notice new cognitive difficulties, find out immediately if your parent has been given any new medications.
3. Entertainment is a critical part of your parent's journey. Make sure they have plenty to keep them busy. This will keep them happy and you happier.

## *Excerpt from a Nursing Report:*

*They had found my mother, dressed up, sitting in her wheelchair outside the front doors. When asked what she was doing out there, she replied that she was waiting for Saddam Hussein to pick her up for their dinner date.*

# Chapter 8
## Nursing Home Issues: A Day in the Life

### They're Coming to Take Me Away, Ha Ha, Hee Hee

Thinking about the nursing home as an "institution" is a recipe for guilt. The connotation for institution, at least for me, elicits thoughts of a mental institution complete with little white men in their little white coats. The nursing home is another step along the journey through old age. If your parent needs help cooking and cleaning, assisted living can help. If your parent needs help dressing and using the bathroom, a nursing home can help. It's not a dirty word and doesn't have to be a dirty place.

Many guidelines exist in choosing a nursing home. You can find many resources in the library or online about how to choose. After reading the guidelines and following the recommendations, my advice after narrowing down the selection is to go by the golden rule: do unto others as you would have them do unto you. Choose a nursing home that you would be comfortable staying in yourself, when that time comes. Visit them not only at prearranged times, but at unexpected times to make sure that you see the whole picture.

I didn't have the luxury of researching many choices. My mother was in the hospital when the individual responsible for arranging discharge contacted me. She gave me two choices of nursing homes close to the hospital. One accepted Medicaid and one did not. Although we never required Medicaid, at the time I thought it would be prudent to go with the one that accepted it.

We got lucky. The nursing home I chose was a wonderful place, with caring and loving people and an effective nursing staff. It is a place that neither my husband nor I will mind going to at the end of our journey.

*For your own sake, don't call the nursing home an institution. Choose a nursing home wisely after knowing all the facts. Find a place that you would be comfortable staying in and calling home.*

## Roommates

When my mother first entered the nursing home, she felt too weak to do anything but lay in bed. As her recovery progressed, her sleep patterns returned to normal. And with them, her snoring, moaning, and other nighttime noises returned. Her roommate couldn't sleep through the noise and requested to have her moved. I understood. When Mom stayed at our house, my eight month old puppy barked at her nighttime noises and wouldn't stop until I put on an air cleaner to mask the sounds.

My mother's next roommate was deaf and on oxygen. That solved the nighttime noises problem. At first, the match worked. After my mother recovered enough to want socialization, however, it frustrated her having no one she could talk to. At her request, they moved her to another room.

Marian was a wonderful and gentle soul who never had a bad word to say about anybody. She had suffered a stroke several years before, which left one arm useless and confined her to a wheelchair. She tolerated my mother's petty complaints far longer than I would have expected. My mother, since she was more mobile, did help Marian whenever she could. Sometimes, when neither of them could reach the nurse call button, my mother would go into the hallway to bring back a nurse to help Marian. So it wasn't until the nursing home reorganized their layout that Marian and my mother moved to separate rooms.

My mother moved into the new room before her new roommate, Violet. At the time, I thought that was the problem. I thought my mother became possessive because she had the room a couple days longer. When Violet moved in, the quarrels started immediately. Mainly, it was my mother who complained about everything, and poor Violet had to take it.

Now that I look back on the situation, I think I understand what the problem was. When Violet moved in, she brought with her a large easy chair. Normally this wouldn't have been an issue, as the room was more than large enough to accommodate it. Unfortunately, the placement of the chair caused the problem. My mother loved her clothes. The social worker had crowned her "best dressed" at the nursing home, and my mother lived up to it every day. She spent many hours picking out the following day's clothes, checking out her clothes, and arranging her clothes. The easy chair was placed in front of her closet. A nurse could fit in the space easily to get clothes out for her, but that didn't satisfy my mother. She had to get them herself, and her wheelchair wouldn't fit behind the easy chair.

She did complain about this, but since no one involved realized the extent of my mother's obsession with her clothes, they all ignored it. Since someone could fit back there to access her closet, they thought that was good enough. I think if we had been more aware of where my mother was coming from, it might have relieved the situation.

As it was, tensions ran high and my mother was on her worst behavior. She constantly bickered with Violet and spoke to her gruffly. More than once I had to remove my mother from the room forcibly because I couldn't take her continual abuse of the poor woman. Once I had to leave because my mother wouldn't stop. I even apologized to Violet who was more understanding than she should have been.

Finally, they honored my mother's demands for a new room. I was glad because I couldn't stand how she treated her roommate. Nothing I could say would stop my mother from further abuse.

They moved her into a four-person room with only one other person. This woman, a little on the abusive side herself, used to park herself in front of the door and wouldn't let my mother come in or go out. When asked to move out of the way, she shouted curses. They moved her out after awhile and my mother had the big four-person room all to herself, which she loved.

Eventually they moved someone else in. This person slept in a fetal position ninety-nine per cent of the time, only getting up for meals and trips to the bathroom. You'd think there would be nothing to complain about, but every once in awhile, my mother would find something. Mostly, though, the arrangement worked.

Many nursing home residents become distressed with room moves, so they are usually limited. Once a resident settles into their own space, normally they want to stay there. But in a case like my mother's, where there are problems or abuse present, then the move is best for all parties involved.

*If your parent complains of a roommate issue, try to discover any underlying problems not readily apparent. Look for something that is important to your parent that everyone may have overlooked. If your parent becomes agitated after a room move, understand that his or her world has been disrupted and act accordingly. Your parent needs your support.*

Yours, Mine, and Ours
The problems with stealing began almost immediately. Shortly after my mother was aware enough to know what was going on, she discovered that her wallet and fifteen dollars were missing from her purse. Since I never checked the purse after she went to the hospital, it's possible the money and wallet were stolen from there.

Unfortunately, it gave my mother a fear of stealing. When she shared the room with Violet, she accused her of stealing her clothes. Violet was confined to her wheelchair or her bed, and she wore a different size. But since my mother couldn't access her closet to reassure herself that her clothes were still there, she told me that Violet had stolen them. She also announced it to everyone else who would listen.

I received a call from the social worker concerned about my mother's accusations. She was unhappy about her telling the world about the theft when she didn't feel there was any. She said I needed to get her to stop saying that. I felt like a mother receiving a phone call that their kid had been bad in school. Maybe this was payback for the trouble I caused while in I was in school! Regardless, the situation troubled me.

Nothing I said dampened her accusations against poor Violet. My mother insisted Violet stole the clothes. I tried to explain it in reasonable terms, that Violet wore a different size, and the clothes were still in my mother's own closet. Nothing made a difference. Asking her to stop making those comments was useless, and I begged her to start behaving. Yelling at her made me feel bad. Yet, it worked when nothing else did. The situation finally resolved itself when they moved my mother to another room.

Periodically she'd complain that some item of clothing was missing, and then a nurse or I would find it. Once she told me that she had found an eyebrow pencil that she thought was stolen. It had been under a magazine in her drawer. My mother always wanted me to bring her candy or cookies a couple at a time, instead of by the box. She said she didn't want to pay for other people eating them all the time.

Shortly after she got a new roommate, she started on the stealing thing again. She told me the night before she had put out a towel and a bra and underwear, and when she awoke in the morning, it was gone. Although she did say that she wasn't sure that someone had taken it, she added that she would try it again to see if they disappeared again. Then she told me that when she woke up in the morning, she already had her clothes on. I said, "Mom, if you had your clothes on, that's where your underwear disappeared!" Still not convinced, she grumbled.

On another occasion, I asked my mother about some oranges and grapefruit that I had brought her a couple days before. She told me they were gone because someone had taken them. Later in the conversation, she mentioned there was a bag of oranges and grapefruit on the other side of the room with someone else's belongings. Her roommate had left some time before, and she had been alone for over a month. I tried to explain that to her, and that those were the same ones that she lost. She said she didn't want them if they weren't hers. Finally, after some convincing, she believed me.

A friend told me that her elderly aunt, taken care of by nurses in her own home, always accused the help of stealing things, especially after someone new was hired. Another friend told me that her mother, who lived by herself in her own home, still worried about the loss of her things. She would hide her purse in her walker and keep it with her all the time! No strangers ever came to the house, so it was an unrealistic fear. So it's not isolated to nursing home life.

In the believe it or not department, this next incident really shocked me. My mother called one night crunching on something as we talked. I asked her what she was crunching on. She said crackers that she thought she had gotten out of her own nightstand. When she came into her room, she became confused about which bed was hers. That was understandable as each bed looked similar with the same nightstand next to each one. She went over to the bed that she thought was hers and found some crackers on the nightstand. She said she also found candy there and thought that I had left it for her. Although she said that she thought the crackers were hers, she also mentioned that she thought they might be her roommate's. The whole time we talked she kept crunching. Since the beds and the nightstands were about thirty feet apart, I kept asking how close to her telephone the nightstand was. I eventually got her to realize they were the roommate's crackers, but she still kept eating them. Finally I convinced her to put them back and to tell her roommate that I would buy her some new ones. I couldn't believe that my mother didn't know what side of the room her bed was on, but the more we talked I realized how confused she was. Also shocking, was that she was so obsessed with stealing and yet she did it herself, although unintentionally. This distressing incident again proved that I was not dealing with my original mom, whose honesty had always been impeccable.

*In hospitals, nursing homes, even assisted living apartments—anyplace with people coming and going all the* **time** *—there is always the possibility of theft. Often though, an item is misplaced. Always be understanding and try to find the lost item without being judgmental.*

Report Card Day
	When my mother went from her one hundred days of Medicare to private pay, she had to have a state ordered evaluation.  This assessment measures the person's ability to care of themselves.  The criteria the state guidelines are based on include "Activities of Daily Living":

1. Bed mobility:  being able to turn over and move freely in bed.
2. Transfer:  getting in and out of bed, getting in and out of a wheelchair, etc.
3. Toilet:  being able to use the restroom without assistance.
4. Locomotion:  moving around the floor without assistance, wheelchair is acceptable, if they can put it in motion by themselves.
5. Eating:  from fork to mouth; this does not include having the food ground up, which doesn't count against them.

	Someone "qualifies" for nursing home care if they require three out of five extensive assists.  Or, with cognitive impairment, two limited assists plus the cognitive problems qualify.  If a person does not require these assists, then they might qualify for "residential care" or "boarding home level."  Residential care within a nursing home is similar to assisted living.  Their bed linens are changed, someone gives them their medicine, and they are given meals, but they manage their own day to day lives.
	The reason a state contracted agency does the evaluations is so you can get an outside objective opinion.  What if you think your parent can take care of themselves enough for residential care, but the nursing home insists that your parent

needs nursing home level? Who is right? An outside agency hired by the state solves this problem. They have the final say, although if your parent is on Medicaid you can appeal if you think they're wrong.

In my mother's case, we eagerly awaited the results of her evaluation, because we thought she could transfer to the residential level, which would have been significantly less expensive. Unfortunately, she didn't qualify. Although I felt disappointed, it didn't surprise me that much. More than that, it confirmed my earlier decision of letting her apartment go. If she could take care of herself enough for residential level, then it would follow that she could probably live in her own apartment. Luckily I didn't have to deal with the guilt that might have brought.

When my mother had a three-day stay in the hospital for severe congestive heart failure, she again qualified for Medicare for a short time. After Medicare ended, she needed the evaluation again. Anytime there is an interruption in service, an evaluation is required.

The inherent problem with the concept is that often seniors don't want to admit they need assistance. They want to hold on to their independence for as long as they can. My mother, for example, always tried her hardest to prevail over any challenges that came her way. If someone asked her if she could get to the bathroom by herself, even if she had never done it, she'd do everything in her power to accomplish that task. Problem was, she couldn't do it every time. It's a good idea if you can be there with your parent during the evaluation. Then, if your parent tries to present themselves as Superman when they're only Mighty Mouse, you can make sure the whole truth comes out.

> *The evaluation agency will give an objective view of your parent that you may not be able to see yourself. Be there for the evaluation and then get a copy of their report, which should include how many hours per day your parent needs assistance.*

<u>Guilt Excursions Sold Here</u>
During another of my mother's hospital stays, I received a call from the evaluation agency. Per the agency's latest assessment, my mother qualified for nursing home care. The woman from the agency explained that my mother told her she was hoping to get into the assisted living part of the nursing home. Along with the regular report, the woman said she would send information on homecare. I told her that my mother has more confidence in her abilities than she should have, and that she has cognitive problems that would preclude her living alone.

It was a guilt-producing phone call. Once again I had to wonder if I was making the right decision to keep my mother in a nursing home and prevent her from going to her own apartment. Luckily, I didn't have to feel guilty for too long.

My mother called less than ten minutes after I hung up with the agency. She laughed and said that she had "a little mishap" the night before. She explained that she had gotten up in the middle of the night on the wrong side of the bed. Literally on the wrong side of the bed. On one side of her bed the wheelchair waits for her to get in and out of it. On the other side of the bed, there is a rail to prevent her from getting out on the wrong side. But my creative and persistent mother crawled to the bottom of the bed farther than the rails extend. She said that she knew her wheelchair was on the other side. But she figured since she was already there, she might as well go. After taking the three steps she thought would take her to the bathroom, she sat down on the toilet. But she had misjudged, and the toilet was still far away. My mother told me that she fell to the floor and landed in a "pile of pee." Since she couldn't get up, she had to wait until the nurse heard her calling out.

This again demonstrated that my mother did not have the capacity to recognize her limitations. Not only did she miscalculate the distance to the bathroom (more like ten steps from that side of the bed), but she also misjudged her ability to walk that far. There was no way she was capable of living on her own. Usually my mother was adept at handing out guilt trips. This time, she canceled my mine!

*Sometimes your perception of your parent is more accurate than how they portray themselves to other people. Do what you think is best for the safety of your parent.*

## House Calls

Something to consider when choosing a nursing home is if they take patients to routine doctor's appointments. If your parent is already in a nursing home, check the information packet you received on admittance. A friend became stressed out over a situation like this.

Her father, a stroke patient, had a doctor's appointment. The head nurse called her and asked her if she could take her father to the appointment. My friend who worked full time and had a family to take care of, couldn't see how she could find the time. She didn't want her father to miss his appointment, and she had no idea why they were asking her to take him. With the monthly cost so high, she thought doctor's appointments should be included.

She finally arranged for a volunteer senior group to take him and pick him up. Everything seemed fine until she received a call from the doctor's nurse. The nurse told her how badly it had been handled. It wasn't the senior group's fault. They do the driving and are not equipped to help a barely ambulatory man into and out of a car. The clinic had to do that, and it was an unsatisfactory scene. Her father luckily didn't realize the problem, but the nurse was furious the nursing home didn't handle the situation themselves. My friend commented that at those prices, trips to the doctor should be included.

After that episode, much stress, and coaching from her friends, she finally questioned the nursing home about why it wasn't included. Their answer was that they only had one vehicle for field trips and required doctor's visits, and with all their residents, they depended on family members to help out when they could. My friend, livid and stressed out even more, felt there was nothing she could do about it.

A few weeks later as she was going through her informational packet looking for a Medicare date, she found a document titled Description of Items and Services Covered under Daily rate. Guess what was there! The nursing home was responsible for transportation of the residents to routine doctor's appointments!

The nursing home that my mother was at always managed to get her to her various doctor's visits. Once when she had to be hospitalized for a day, a nurse who had befriended my mother picked her up from the hospital in her own car. Sometimes caring people can make a huge impact on your life and the life of your parent.

*Routine doctor's appointments are an integral part of your parent's stay in a nursing home. Make sure that their services include transportation to routine appointments.*

<u>Meetings</u>

The nursing home conducts several meetings during the year. Some of them are state mandated. They may have different names in different nursing homes.

Quarterly Care meetings, regulated by the state, are most important for family involvement. The state requires nursing facilities to invite family members once per year. Some nursing homes, like the one my mother was in, encourage family members to come quarterly. In the first Quarterly Care meeting that I went to, they discussed my mother's coughing problem. I had always believed that she had a problem with milk products and I mentioned it at the meeting. They limited her milk products and it helped her coughing tremendously.

The Quarterly Care meeting is important not only for what you can add about your parent, but the information they can give you about your parent. Representatives from five different departments are there. The social worker from social services talks about how well your parent is adjusting, how he or she gets along with others, and roommate issues. Someone from nursing discusses any medical or medication problems, and any nursing related issues. The person from dietary tells about any eating related problems or dietary issues, such as if your parent is gaining or losing weight. If your parent is getting rehabilitation therapy, then someone from rehab will be there to talk about that. And finally, someone from the activities department will be there. This person tells whether your parent takes advantage of the daily activities. The activities person probably knows the true nature of your parent more than anyone else at the meeting. During their time together your parent has fun. There are few or no stresses during activities, and everyone wants to have a good time. Hearing about your parent having a good time makes everyone happy.

Residential Council serves the residents of the nursing home as a place to air their grievances. This is the place for the residents to discuss things they want more of, things they want less of, things they like, and things they don't like. In these meetings they discuss activities, food service, and nursing issues. Sometimes the heads of other departments speak at the meetings. Someone distributes the minutes of the meeting to all departments involved in the discussions. These meetings are valuable to nursing home residents. The nursing home is their world, and this is their chance to be heard and to make positive changes.

Family Council meetings are probably different everywhere. Often they have speakers on different subjects of interest for residents' family members. The meeting that I went to on Medicare/Medicaid was informative and worthwhile.

*Make sure you attend all Quarterly Care meetings (if invited), and encourage your parent to go to the Residential Council meetings. Watch for subjects of interest at the Family Council meetings.*

Impact of Others

Many accounts of nursing homes speak of people reaching out to you in hallways as you go by. That didn't happen at the nursing home my mother was in. However, I was affected by other residents.

One time when I visited my mother, the woman in the bed across from hers had a gentleman caller. It didn't take long to realize that he was a minister. As I sat there chit-chatting with my mother and clipping her toenails, the minister asked the woman if she felt she was at the end of her life. There I sat, engaged in a pitifully mundane task, while this woman contemplated her own death. Overhearing that conversation made me feel incredibly small and insignificant.

Another short-term roommate of my mother's came to the nursing home sometime after breaking her hip. The whole time I visited I heard her pleas for help. Over and over again she called out to God. First she'd ask for his help, then she'd ask for him to take her. She said, "How can I be happy when I have to live like this?" Her pain must have been overwhelming. They gave her medication, but probably not enough to eliminate the pain completely. This went on for some time until they moved her to another section of the facility. It was disconcerting hearing her pleading with God.

One of my mother's early roommates, Marian, was a sweetheart. In the short time my mother shared a room with her, Marian and I became very close. When Marian and my mother both moved to other rooms, I'd still stop in and see Marian. Also, they still shared a table in the dining room, and Marian would always kiss and hug me when she saw me. So it was with deep regret and sad surprise when I found out that Marian had died unexpectedly. At first, I couldn't stop thinking about her. Every time I walked into the nursing home, it felt so empty without her there. I'd walk past her door and flinch when I saw her name missing. What bothered me the most is that I had never told her how much I loved her. I hope she knows now.

*Other residents living in the nursing home can have an unexpected impact on you. Sometimes it's good, sometimes it's bad. But it's all part of the experience.*

### When She Was Skilled

Toward the end of my mother's stay at the nursing home, she went from "skilled care" to residential care. The residential care was a type of assisted living arrangement inside the nursing home. She had wanted to make that move from early on, but several things prevented it. When we first wanted to move her over there, the contracted agency who did the assessment graded her nursing home level. Although it surprised me, there wasn't much I could do. Some time later, she was assessed again after a hospital stay, and they graded her residential level. At the time an opening did occur, my mother had finally found a living situation that she was happy with, and I didn't want to spoil it by moving her into a new situation.

Eventually circumstances dictated that she should move into the residential section. My mother had become unhappy with her roommate, and thought she was paying too much where she was. She said that she didn't need nurses and she wanted to be more independent. After checking her records, everyone agreed she should move, and luckily there was an opening. So, they told her that she was moving to the residential section.

She called me up wanting me to come over there. I knew that her possessions would be moved for her, as they were in the past, so I told her no. Then she started picking a fight with me on another subject. I told her I didn't want to talk about it. So she brought up something else to fight about. After four different items came up that she wanted to fight about, I decided it would be best to get off the phone.

Two days later my mother called me, already in her new room and happy as could be. She went on and on about her beautiful new room, the new and better dining room that she ate in, and her new privileges. She beamed with happiness.

The next time I went to see her I ran into the Activities Director, Lydia. We talked about how happy my mother was in her new room, and I told her about the fight she had picked with me the day she moved. Lydia told me that although my mother had fought to move over there, when it happened the reality of it frightened her. She was so used to being taken care of and having nurses around all the time, this new move was way out of her comfort zone. I was glad that Lydia could see both sides of the situation and explain about my mother's aberrant behavior.

> *Remember how stressful and traumatic even simple moves can feel to an aging parent. It may seem simple to us, but not in their rapidly shrinking world. The input the nursing home staff can give you at times like this is priceless. They can help you understand a confusing situation or why your parent is acting in a particular way.*

## To Tell the Truth

Several months before the end of my mother's stay at the nursing home, she was taken to the emergency room for congestive heart failure. During the diagnostic process, they took a chest x-ray which showed a small tumor in her lung. A CT scan confirmed that she had lung cancer.

I declined for her to receive any chemo or radiation therapy and asked the next natural question. How long does she have? The doctor said it was a slow growing tumor and it could be a year or more. Since she had a serious heart condition, I asked if it was possible that it might not impact her life? He said it might not. After further discussion we both agreed it was better not to tell my mother. If and when she started exhibiting symptoms or asking questions, then we could tell her. It concerned me that someone at the nursing home might divulge the information to her, and I told him that I would prefer he or I tell her than someone else. He agreed, but said he didn't think that was anything to worry about.

Although he did write it on the hospital release papers, I figured that since it was one line amongst many, it might get overlooked.

Shortly after this, I had a Medicare meeting with the social worker at the nursing home. After the official part finished, we continued talking about other topics. I felt close to her and enjoyed our discussions. The lung cancer issue tore me up. Although I wanted to confide in her, I didn't know how her official duties fit in and I still didn't want my mother to find out accidentally. So I decided not to say anything, although our discussion included end of life issues.

Early the next week, I had to call the social worker to find out about physical therapy for my mother. After answering my question, she inquired about the lung cancer. I explained my reasons for not telling her, but still felt badly about it. She said that I should have discussed it with staff and told them that I didn't want my mother to know. As it was, there was a chance that someone may have inadvertently said something in front of her, not knowing it was supposed to be kept a secret.

The social worker also told me that my mother had told the physical therapist that she "had a disease, now," but didn't elaborate on it. My feeling was that if she knew about it, she would disparage me for not telling her. The old mom would try to protect me by not mentioning it to me, but the new mother didn't think that way.

>Don't keep secrets from the nursing home staff! Or a home nursing staff, especially if they have access to your parent's records. They can handle any medical situations much better if they know what is going on.

\* \* \* \* \*

## Points to Remember:

1. For your own sake, don't call the nursing home an institution. Choose a nursing home wisely after knowing all the facts. Find a place that you would be comfortable staying in and calling home.

2. If your parent complains of a roommate issue, try to discover any underlying problems not readily apparent. Look for something that is important to your parent that everyone may have overlooked. If your parent becomes agitated after a room move, understand that his or her world has been disrupted and act accordingly. Your parent needs your support.

3. In hospitals, nursing homes, even assisted living apartments—anyplace with people coming and going all the time—there is always the possibility of theft. Often though, an item is misplaced. Always be understanding and try to find the lost item without being judgmental.

4. The evaluation agency will give an objective view of your parent that you may not be able to see yourself. Be there for the evaluation and then get a copy of their report, which should include how many hours per day your parent needs assistance.

5. Sometimes your perception of your parent is more accurate than how they portray themselves to other people. Do what you think is best for the safety of your parent.

6. Routine doctor's appointments are an integral part of your parent's stay in a nursing home. Make sure that their services include transportation to routine appointments.

7. Make sure you attend all Quarterly Care meetings (if invited), and encourage your parent to go to the Residential Council meetings. Watch for subjects of interest at the Family Council meetings.

8. Other residents living in the nursing home can have an unexpected impact on you. Sometimes it's good, sometimes it's bad. But it's all part of the experience.

9. Remember how stressful and traumatic even simple moves can feel to an aging parent. It may seem simple to us, but not in their rapidly shrinking world. The input the nursing home staff can give you at times like this is priceless. They can help you understand a confusing situation or why your parent is acting in a particular way.

10. Don't keep secrets from the nursing home staff! Or a home nursing staff, especially if they have access to your parent's records. They can handle any medical situations much better if they know what is going on.

*Excerpt from My Journal:*
*Mom told me that she was hanging out with one of her friends and the friend asked her if she had a Kleenex. When Mom said yes, the friend told her that she had a drop hanging off her nose. Mom told her that she didn't even know it was there. And the friend said, "That's what friends are for."*

*Excerpt from an Email to a Friend:*
*I went to a Quarterly Meeting at the nursing home yesterday. There were six people in the meeting, from the occupational therapists to the activities director, and everyone raved about her.*

She has made quite an impact there. She has become an "advocate of patient's rights" and absolutely demands them. Everyone is glad that she is there and that she has made a positive difference in the place.

## Chapter 9
## The Home Alternative: Ain't No Place Like Home

<u>Finding Ole Saint Nick</u>
Finding someone appropriate to take care of your aging parent can be the stuff of nightmares. While you're searching for someone kind and gentle like Santa Claus, you may be finding life's castaways, who are looking for a place to live. Even in a large city where there is more of a selection, finding the quality person who you are looking for is difficult. Most families go through several caregivers before finding the right one.

My friend told me what a disaster it was finding someone to take care of her mother. Many of the women had drinking or emotional problems that weren't apparent when she interviewed them. She didn't even realize the extent of the problems until after the women had moved into the house. There was even suspicions of one woman being abusive to her mother. But the emotional upheaval that she went through trying to find someone left her anxious and worried. After a long string of failed attempts, my friend finally found someone wonderful to care for her mother.

When I thought about getting someone to stay with my mother instead of letting her stay in a nursing home, many factors affected my decision.

Once I found a suitable person to stay with her, who would take care of her on weekends? What if the weekly person became sick? What if the person hurt her back while helping my mother up—what liability would we be facing? If you go through an agency, many of these problems disappear, but then you lose the ability to choose someone individually.

I think it's important that you know yourself. Since I worked full time, I knew I couldn't substitute if someone got sick. Also, I know I need some rest on the weekends or I can't go on. Perhaps this is a personal fault. But at least I can recognize my limitations and not fool myself into thinking that I can do something that I cannot. That would not be good for my mother or me.

> *Finding someone to care for your parent is never easy. If this is the path you choose, remain diligent and hopeful and the right person will turn up. Carefully consider all the implications before you take this step.*

## Misinterpreting the Situation

A woman I know called her mother on Mother's Day, and her mother never answered the phone. After some frantic phone calls to people her mother knew, she found her at the hospital with a minor injury. Since her mother had been on her own before, the woman thought that besides a little company and occasional help, her mother should be able to live alone with no problem. When someone came over to do some housecleaning, they found a glass of orange juice on the floor. Her mother had dropped it and couldn't pick it up. Another time she found a pint of ice cream left out of the refrigerator.

After the hospital incident and the other inconsistencies, her mother had moved into an apartment across the street from her. Although it quickly became obvious that her mother could not function on her own, her main concern was whether the move to unfamiliar surroundings caused her mother to deteriorate so rapidly. She couldn't move her mother back to where she had lived, and yet the deterioration wore heavily on her mind. She had talked to her mother every day before the move, and hadn't picked up any clues that she was declining. The situation confused and depressed her.

As the situation progressed, she and her husband realized they didn't know what they had gotten themselves into. Her mother was much worse off than she had expected, which required a change of plans. After realizing that her mother couldn't take care of herself in her own apartment, my friend and her husband began searching for a new home the three of them could share.

*For your parents' sake and your own sake, make sure you know exactly how much assistance they will need before introducing any changes into their lives.*

## Someone Else to Think About

Sometimes the parent having the problems isn't the only person involved. That parent may have a spouse directly affected by any decisions. The spouse may be the one who determines the correct course of action.

A friend's mother was severely impacted with dementia. It came on slowly at first and became more severe over time. Gertrude's father, as his duties changed, grew angrier and angrier. He had to give up his gardening so he could do the cooking and cleaning. Because he couldn't leave her alone, he also had to give up his part-time carpentry business. Since he was getting older, too, he would have eventually had to give up those activities anyway. But because the mother needed extra care, their roles changed and he was not happy about it.

Gertrude's mother had been in and out of the hospital several times for various problems. When released, she spent time in a nursing home for rehabilitation purposes. One of those times, Gertrude told her father that she didn't think her mother could come home. She asked her father what he thought about that. His response was, "Well, if she can't walk, I don't know how I can take care of her."

After her mother had settled into the nursing home, Gertrude found her father less angry than he had been in a long time. Having his wife at home had made life difficult for him. Gertrude said that once her mother was in the nursing home, her father's life changed. It was not so burdened or stressful. He could finally relax. It had been good for him.

Gertrude said occasionally she still debates with herself and her sister about moving her mother back home. But the additional care it would require, and the stress for her father, would not work out. She said that most of the time, her mother forgets that she's even in a nursing home. The only time she talks about going home is after she visits with Gertrude's father. Gertrude thinks it triggers something in her mother like, "Oh, I have a husband. I should be home taking care of him. I should get home." But since her mother doesn't retain anything, five minutes after he leaves, she's content again. Gertrude also said that if her mother was begging to go home, she would have a much harder time of it.

*When you make these decisions about your parents, arrange it so there are positive effects for everyone involved.*

## Out of Control

After taking care of your parent at home for any length of time, one issue of having them in a nursing home is the loss of control. One woman I spoke to said that she had fed her mother, cut her hair, cleaned up after her, bathed her, and that she knew every mark on her body. Suddenly, after moving her to a nursing home, she didn't know what she had for breakfast or if she was feeling well. For so long she had done all of those things, and now she was a bystander. She felt guilty that she didn't know the details. It became a real struggle within her until she realized that she didn't need to know the details anymore. The process felt difficult to get through.

Even though I wasn't taking care of my mom at the time she had her stroke, the loss of control had a huge impact on me. Not only was the whole stroke episode hard to deal with, but not knowing the outcome was a real killer. I didn't know where it was all going, but I did know there was nothing I could do about it. It was out of my control. That was the hard part. You want so much to keep everything normal; you want so much to have everything the way it was.

*If you have had total control over your parents' life, and then find them transferred to a medical or nursing home facility, it is difficult to give up the control that you once had. As your parents age and have health issues that affect their life, you may often feel out of control. Try to accept the changes and deal with it the best way that you can.*

<u>Decision Time</u>
Sometimes, usually after a health crisis, a decision is made to move a parent from a home situation to a nursing home. And sometimes that doesn't work out. Such was the case with my friend, Lily. Her mother-in-law, Marie, spent several days in the hospital, and then was transferred to a nursing home for rehabilitation. Lily and her husband had decided, because of the health incident, that it was time for Marie to live in the nursing home instead of maintaining her own home.

Every day Marie would call her son and say, "I need to come home, I can't be here. You have to come and get me and take me home!" After Marie finished the rehabilitation, she did get stronger, and Lily and her husband had to reconsider their decision.

They knew that Marie was a strong woman and that she knew what she wanted. They finally realized that if she was going to be that unhappy and that miserable, then they might as well let her go home. If she fell and broke something, so be it, because she'd rather die at home than in the nursing home.

This was written four years after Marie moved back home, and she's still bright and perky and going strong. As Lily said, "Sometimes you have to step back and say, it's not what I want, it's what's best for them."

*Sometimes you need to re-evaluate decisions made during or directly after a medical crisis. Older people often have an amazing capacity for recovery.*

<u>I've Fallen and I Can't Get Up</u>
Many times when an aging parent is in their own home or spends time alone in yours, having an emergency response system can save a life. But sometimes it doesn't work out the way it was intended. My friend Marsha left her mother home alone during the day while she was at work. She felt comfortable doing that because her mother wore one of those systems around her neck. One afternoon, Marsha came home to find her mother on the floor, face red and exhausted from trying to get up. She had fallen down and when she tried to use a nearby chair to help her get up, the chair fell down with her. Marsha asked her mother why she didn't press the button. Her mother replied, "I didn't want to disturb you. I thought I could handle it by myself."

Both Lily's father and mother-in-law have an emergency response system attached to their walker. Lily is concerned because if one of them falls down over here and their walker is over there, then it is of no use to them. She said that if they wear it and accidentally hit it, then somebody calls over the little speaker phone. That happened to her father who has a hearing problem. Since he didn't hear them calling, they go down their list of who needs to be contacted if the elderly person can't be reached. After several false alarms when Lily rushed into his house and he demanded, "What's going on? What's the problem?" they decided a good compromise would be attaching it to the walker.

> Recognize if your parent would be the type who would be willing to push the button on an emergency response system. Sometimes having it available isn't enough. It's another important item to consider if you are thinking about home care.

<u>Torn Between Two Loyalties</u>
Which are you first, wife or daughter (or husband or son)? There's not an easy answer to that question. Most women try to do both as best as they can. My friend, Gertrude, found herself in that unfortunate position. While her mother, who suffered from dementia, needed help nightly going to bed, Gertrude's family suffered from her absence. Gertrude had to leave the house about the time when her husband and children came home. She felt it was her duty to take care of her mother, and she knew in her heart that her family would understand. They may have understood intellectually, but they weren't getting their needs met.

The situation threw the whole family off balance, and when they started having problems, Gertrude said she never saw it coming. Of course she never saw it coming! She was too busy caring for her mother and trying to do the right thing! And in her spare time taking care of her family! Too bad there wasn't any time left for Gertrude.

And that's the other side of the story—mother or daughter or person in your own right? The mother or wife who is caregiver for her parent, is always torn between "where should I be" and "what should I be doing now?" The one person always left out of the priority list is the caregiver herself. That's the one person who will never complain that she's not getting enough time. So the struggle is not only juggling parents and family, but also leaving out the all-important "I."

*Your parent may need you desperately, but so does your family. If you don't have help from siblings or other family members, hire someone to help. And don't forget to take care of yourself. If something happens to you, your parent and family will all suffer.*

<u>Waiting for a Sign from Above</u>

A friend had her mother taken care of in a house across the street from where she and her husband lived. She mentioned to me a couple times that she was "waiting for a sign" that she should put her mother into a nursing home. When I asked her about it, she jokingly said that she was waiting for a purple, five hundred pound gorilla to drop onto the hood of her car while holding a sign that says, "Today's the Day!"

My friend said that she gets more strength and she sucks it in and feels like she can go on another day. She said that if she had to be the primary caregiver, then it probably would have been time a long time ago. But since it's not a twenty-four hour proposition for her, she is able to recharge and keep it going.

She acknowledged they may be stretching a situation they shouldn't have stretched. She keeps thinking that her mother will have to go back into the hospital and won't be able to come out. That's the type of sign she thinks will eventually come.

What she was looking for was something that was so apparent that it left no doubt which direction to take. My friend is taking care of her mother at home, and she constantly wonders if she's doing the right thing. I have my mother in a pleasant and qualified nursing home, and I constantly wonder if I'm doing the right thing. Where parents are concerned and so many factors involved, I'm not sure if you can ever feel confident about your decisions.

There are probably many "signs" along the way, but it is up to you to follow them. I think it's more something that you need to be ready for, rather than your parent. There's no harm in that. Keep everything comfortable for you and your parent.

* * * * *

<u>Points to Remember:</u>

1. Finding someone to care for your parent is never easy. If this is the path you choose, remain diligent and hopeful and the right person will turn up. Carefully consider all the implications before you take this step.

2. For your parent's sake and your own sake, make sure you know exactly how much assistance they will need before introducing any changes into their lives.

3. When you make these decisions about your parents, try to arrange it so there are positive effects for everyone involved.

4. If you have had total control over your parents' life, and then find them transferred to a medical or nursing home facility, it is difficult to give up the control that you once had. As your parents age and have health issues that affect their life, you may often feel out of control. Try to accept the changes and deal with it the best way that you can.

5. Sometimes decisions made during or directly after a medical crisis need to be re-evaluated. Older people often have an amazing capacity for recovery.

6. Recognize if your parent would be the type who would be willing to push the button on an emergency response system. Sometimes having it available isn't enough. It's another important item to consider if you are thinking about home care.

7. Your parent may need you desperately, but so does your family. If you don't have help from siblings or other family members, hire someone to help. And don't forget to take care of yourself. If something happens to you, your parent and family will all suffer.

8. There are probably many "signs" along the way, but it is up to you to follow them. I think it's more something that you need to be ready for, rather than your parent. There's no harm in that. Keep everything comfortable for you and your parent.

*Excerpt from an Interview:*

There were times when it's really hard to juggle and balance, work and home life, and husbands and kids and still try to help them at the same time. You just sort of fit it into your schedule and do the best you can. I can't say I've done it all right, I can't say I've done it all really well. But we've gotten through it. It's hard to do it all. You do the best you can and you do what you gotta do.

I don't really want it to be over, I mean I want rest and peace, but I know that rest and peace is only going to come when she's dead. So I don't want that.

## Chapter 10
## Gifts: Lies and Lessons My Mother Taught Me

### Your Truth, My Truth

A friend of mine told me this sad story about how her aging mother had insulted her so badly that she curled up in a ball and had a hard time coming out of it. Since I considered myself somewhat of an "expert" on difficult and abusive aging parents, I wrote her a long letter. In the letter, I went over many things about her mother that she had told me in the past, as well as current things about her. And then I gave her what I felt was excellent advice.

Shortly after that, she wrote me back thanking me and saying that not all of it applied. Although I knew that I should not spend any time or energy "defending my viewpoint," I went back over the letter I had written her to see which part could possibly not have applied. The conclusion I came to was if she did not see where it applied, then she was not in touch with her feelings. Period. Luckily I kept that to myself.

Two days later my mother taught me the truth. When I came to visit her, I noticed that her roommate who always spent all her time in the room wasn't there. My mother said with disdain that she left to watch the canoe races. Then we got involved in other matters, and I didn't think any more about it until the roommate returned.

The excited roommate bubbled over at how much fun she had. My mother went on and on about how she would not want to see them, and how she couldn't see why anyone would want to see them. Her roommate answered defensively that she had been looking at someone in the race. At that, my mother conceded that if she had someone to look for, maybe it wouldn't be so bad. But then she countered by asking me what I thought of the canoe races. I answered by saying that I would like to watch them, but I'd even more like to do them. She grabbed that and ran with it, by saying, yes, doing them, but watching them is nothing. Then she babbled on for several minutes about how could anyone in their right mind watch such crap. Although I didn't feel involved in the debate, I still felt like an idiot because of the way she talked. I'm sure the roommate felt that way, too. My mother, so certain that her assessment was correct, abused everyone who didn't think exactly her way. It was so blatantly obvious that she assumed that her truth was everyone's truth. And she was wrong.

Driving home that day, I found it so pitiful that my mother couldn't see that her truth did not apply to everyone else. That's when it hit me. I was just like her! I had been so smug in accusing my friend of not being in touch with her feelings because she hadn't agreed with me. It never occurred to me that perhaps everything that I wrote in that letter really didn't apply to her. I was learning that many aspects of my mother's personality that I didn't like, had already become aspects of my personality. And I didn't even know.

### Adjectives

How my mother loved adjectives and labels. She never lost an opportunity to use them. She referred to a nurse who worked at the nursing home as the fat woman with the triangular butt. Every time she saw someone who didn't look exactly like she thought they should, she made a derogatory comment. As much as this appalled me, I realized that while I may not do that now, I was guilty of it in the past.

Years before, I had told my friend, Lucy, a story about another friend. I referred to my other friend as my "prostitute friend," because she had once, long ago, been a prostitute. Lucy, who had been on crutches since she was a toddler answered, "Oh, am I your crippled friend?" It brought me to my senses. Although I would never refer to anyone with labels such as black, Jewish, or Hispanic, I saw no harm in labeling them prostitute, or tall, or rich, or yes, even crippled. What I didn't realize until Lucy made that comment, was that any label can be just as damaging as an ethnic one. Until my mother's labeling comments about that nurse and other people, I never realized where I learned such poor behavior.

### To Tell the Truth

There was a new person sitting at my mother's table when I wheeled her into the dining room. My mother said to her, "Have you met my daughter? She doesn't give me much time." Since I had enough of her taunting, I leaned over and said very sweetly, "If you keep saying things like that, I'm going to give you even less time." Then I said I loved her and kissed her good-by. As I walked away, I heard her say again, "She doesn't give me much time." I was so furious I could barely contain myself.

The next day when she called me, I asked her why she had said that yesterday. She said because it was the truth. I asked her why she had to say it in front of someone else. She said because it was the truth. I said, "So I can introduce you as my mom, and by the way she's bald, and that would be okay because it's the truth?" She said, "If you think that's all right, then go right ahead." Then I asked her if she thought that she could make me feel guilty so I would come to see her more often. According to her that was not the reason she said it. When I asked her why she did say it, she again said that it was the truth.

There was another woman who sat at her table every day, and I asked my mother how often her children came to visit. They didn't come often. I told my mother that she had made those comments in front of that woman and that her kids rarely came to visit. "So, you made me feel bad and you made her feel bad, too." Acting like she was injured, she said, "Oh, now you're making me feel bad."

What got to me about this whole incident was another realization of how I am like her. How many times have I told people hurtful things with the excuse that "it's the truth"? Then again, sometimes telling someone a truth they can't see for themselves is a gift.

I used to be in an email support group for codependent women. I was mostly a listener, not a participant. One woman constantly complained about her physically abusive husband. The other participants would give her sympathy and soothe her pain. Wouldn't it have been more merciful to tell her that he was not going to change and that she should get some professional help? My mother would have been the person to tell her that.

Telling the truth: sometimes a gift and sometimes just plain mean. My mother never learned the difference. I wasn't sure if I always knew the difference, either.

Balancing the Scales

The nursing home that my mother lived in often had visiting musical entertainers. One time they had a gentleman come in to play the piano. Someone wheeled my mother in to listen. Then her old roommate was wheeled in, but put in the front row. To my mother, this was a terrible insult. For someone to come in after her, but be in front of her wasn't fair. After the concert, the pianist came through the audience talking with people. My mother grabbed his attention and continued talking to him until he had to leave; while her old roommate sat there with her arm in the air trying to get his attention. For my mother, that was the greatest payback she could have hoped for. While her old roommate could sit in the front row, my mother talked to the man—this made it even. Even and fair were everything to her.

Another special day at the nursing home was when they set up plastic pins in the activity room, and the residents used a plastic bowling ball to knock them down. Everyone had a great time—except my mother. She had a complaint. An elderly gentleman with some serious physical problems tried to roll the ball. He could barely hold the ball, let alone roll it down the alley, so he was given several shots at it. My mother said that he had more turns than everyone else. She said, "This game isn't fair."

Yet another way that I found that I am like my mother. However, my mother still hasn't learned the difference between fair and right. It may not have been fair the old gentleman got four turns with the ball. But it was right. I had this illustrated to me years before when a good friend told me a story about her ex-husband. He had caught her with another man and although he had had numerous affairs himself, he was furious. My comment was, "Yeah, but it's only fair." She responded, "But it wasn't right." The person who thought she had all the answers, me, had learned another lesson.

### Nursing Home Crusader

One early morning phone call, my mother told me what had happened at breakfast. Everyone sat at their table waiting for their food, and though the meal cart was right there, no one came to serve the food. They thought someone would come any minute and they waited for a long time. Finally, my mother went looking for someone to ask them to serve breakfast. After she told me this story she said, "I want you to put that in your book!" The following morning, she told them not to forget to give them a waitress again! She was very enamored of herself because she felt like she had saved the day. And she had.

The one thing my mother always did as far back as I can remember is write letters. If she bought a chicken TV dinner and it only had one scrawny piece of chicken in it, she would write them a letter. If she bought a pattern for making a blouse, and the instructions were incorrect or left something out, she would write a letter. She refused to let anything go if there was a way to rectify it.

She passed this trait along to me, and I constantly write letters to politicians and companies and whoever else needs reminding they're not doing what they should be doing. But if you look at this, it is a form of complaining. While my mother was in the nursing home, I read a book whose author said that her mother never complained. With all my mother's many complaints, was I ever jealous! However, there are two ways to look at it. Writing letters that should be written are the positive side of complaining. Constant complaining over trivial matters is annoying. But complaining about things that should be complained about is an art. My mother had it down to a fine science.

During the first Quarterly Care meeting that I attended at the nursing home, everyone raved about my mother. She had become an "advocate for patient rights" and she absolutely demanded them. Many residents never complain even if something is uncomfortable for them. Some of the residents are unable to complain. My mother filled those gaps. I remember her telling me about one nursing helper who picked up the food trays before helping people use the rest room. My mother quickly put a stop to that! Having someone who can speak out and who is willing to speak out is always a benefit for everyone. My mother had made a difference, and everyone recognized it.

## Question Authority

I believe strongly in questioning authority. How do they know? Until I know all the facts so I can decide for myself, I'm not happy. That's why the following is filled with such irony.

My mother always needed everything confirmed by someone with authority. If I told her something, she couldn't be sure about it until someone else confirmed it. For instance, if I told her she should not use salt because of her heart condition, she would say, "Are you a medical doctor?" But if a nurse gave her the same advice, she would listen immediately. This scenario played out all the time. She needed authority to confirm everything.

Until she was in the nursing home and I experienced it constantly, I never realized that I had the same affliction. If my husband told me something, I wouldn't call him a liar, but until someone with more authority confirmed it, I would doubt his words. That's a terrible way to treat someone you love! It felt terrible when my mother did it to me, and it's terrible when I do it to other people. But at least I recognize it now, and that's the first step to correcting a problem.

## Just Kidding

My mother had a great sense of humor and a gift for storytelling. When she mixed the two together, the results could be especially nasty. One afternoon my mother and my brother sat at a neighbor's table and told an unbelievable story. Trouble is, they were such good storytellers the neighbors believed it. Between my youngest brother and myself is a span of ten years. The nasty story told of the ten children that my mother had during those ten years. Detailed descriptions of what was wrong with each child and why it died affected the neighbors so much they had to fight back the tears. Told with practiced straight faces and choking back fake emotions, my mother and brother continued the deception until all ten children had been accounted for. When they walked back across the lawn that day, they giggled under their breath, while the neighbors tried to figure out what had happened to them.

Another incident of "humorous" deceit was when my brother took me horseback riding. When we returned to the house, he wrapped me in ketchup stained rags and carried me into the house to scare my mother. What a terrible joke to play on your mother! But we had learned from the master.

One could argue that people enjoyed hearing stories that horrified or mystified them; that they were in some ways active participants in the deceit. But when the joke turns out to be on them and they had no idea it was coming, that turns it into a hostile and cruel game. Just as it's possible and wrong to tickle a child until it cries, this type of humorous storytelling is not socially acceptable. My mother taught us well, and all her children have participated in this hurtful storytelling. Until someone points out how cruel it can be, it doesn't feel wrong, it feels familiar.

Remember the Alamo
For as long as I can remember, my mother has held grudges. Sometimes small ones, where she will still speak to the person in a rude way. And sometimes large ones, where she will ignore the person at all costs.

None of this stopped when she entered the nursing home. My mother had told me of some incident weeks earlier when a friend of hers had treated her abusively. She wouldn't forget it and let it go. There she was at ninety-three years old, liable to die any minute, and she carried grudges against the very people who made her time there not so lonely.

When I spoke to her she went on and on about two of her woman friends and why she's mad at them. Nothing could convince her that being mad wasn't worth it. Especially now. She wouldn't get that in the end, it would only make her more lonely. She was adamant about no one treating her like that, no matter how long ago the incident occurred. Nothing I would say would change her mind. I always found it amazing that she couldn't remember if she ate breakfast or not, but she could remember some silly event that had happened weeks before. Lesson: Don't carry grudges! And don't be stubborn about it!

## Ain't No River in Egypt

When I get a cold, it always follows the same progression. First I get a sore throat and feel miserable. Then I slowly develop the sniffles until it progresses into a full blown cold. While on the phone with my mom one time before her stroke, I told her my symptoms and said that I was getting a cold. She snapped back, "You're not getting a cold!" I explained these were the same symptoms I had hundreds of times before and it always developed into a cold. "You're not getting a cold," she repeated. I ended the conversation there, because I knew I couldn't convince her otherwise.

My mother never wanted to think the worst. Even if everything pointed in that direction, she would deny the signs. This must have come from not wanting bad things to happen.

Again, this was something I, too, had been guilty of. My husband and I had a dog with a serious illness. We were on a walk one afternoon and my husband noticed the dog wasn't running around with her usual exuberance. I discounted that, thinking she wasn't in the mood to chase squirrels that day. It wasn't until she stood in front of our picture window when a dog walked by and didn't utter a woof, that I finally acknowledged that something was grievously wrong. We took her to the vet barely in time, and after a blood transfusion and many days in doggy intensive care, she survived. My denial of what was happening almost cost her life. Pretending that something bad isn't happening does not make the bad thing go away. Sometimes it makes the bad thing worse.

Don't Blame the Messenger

One of my lessons "inherited" from my mother came from the Activities Director, Lydia. As the three of us sat in an alcove in front of a picture window, we watched squirrels play on the lawn. My mother began complaining about her roommate, who she said watched television during all hours of the night. Since my mother went to sleep at six o'clock, "all hours of the night" could have been seven o'clock. It was difficult to explain to her that watching television at seven or eight or even nine o'clock was reasonable to do. Her response was that if she knew someone was sleeping, she would be nice enough not to do it. (At the same time she saw nothing wrong with setting her loud clock for six o'clock in the morning.)

After I delivered my mother to the dining room to eat breakfast, Lydia and I continued to discuss the situation. We went over everything, including the causes, the possible solutions, and my mother's stubbornness. What Lydia said was that my mother had really high standards, and she got upset if everyone didn't have those same high standards.

An "aha moment" as Oprah would say! The day before I had interviewed for a job and when asked for my weaknesses, my reply was that I had little tolerance for people who were incompetent in their jobs. Oops. I had always been a perfectionist, and if everyone else didn't perform to my self-proclaimed high standards, I got upset, just like my mother. Another lesson learned.

Always Inadequate

The weather warmed up and my mother's wardrobe needed some altering. Because her closet was so small, I needed to take some winter clothes home before I could bring any more summer clothes in. So, I brought two summer blouses and planned to bring more after cleaning out her closet. As soon as she saw what I had brought, she said, "Only two?" I shook my head and said to someone else in the room, "If I would have brought her ten, she would have complained." That was just like my mother. No matter what I did for her, it was never enough.

Shortly after that, I brought her in a load more summer clothes. Later that day, we sat in an alcove enjoying the view from the picture window and talking. As the conversation lagged, my mother said, "I sure could have used those clothes last year." Not once, not when I brought them, not during that conversation, and not when I left for the day, did she ever thank me for bringing them. Saying that she could have used them last year was as close as she got.

It seemed I could never do anything right for my mother. Or perhaps fast enough, or as much as she wanted, or when she wanted, or any of a thousand other things that she could find wrong with what I had done for her. I thought this was a terrible way to make someone feel. No matter what someone did, it was somehow never enough. And it was even worse when I caught myself doing it.

Coincidentally, or maybe not coincidentally at all, shortly after these two events I caught myself making someone else feel this way. My husband, Dan, had brought home a movie for us to watch. He told me what else was available, and I told him that I would have rather watched Harry Potter. The following week, Dan brought home Harry Potter and told me what else was available. At that, I told him that I would have rather watched something else! He didn't respond, and it wasn't until later that I realized what I had done. I apologized many times. Oh no, I'm becoming my mother! At least I realize it, and in realizing and acknowledging it, I can change it.

## You Are What You Wear

My mother had always been proud of her clothes. Very fashion conscious, she would never wear white past Labor Day! She always dressed up, no matter where she was going. Even if she planned to stay home all day, she would dress up in case someone might drop by to visit. The clothes that she made herself provided her with even more pleasure. She loved when anyone told her how beautiful they looked, or how they thought the clothes looked much too professionally done to be handmade. She reveled in all the compliments.

Clothes have never been my thing. Any time I needed to dress up, I let my mother buy me the outfit. For me, shopping for clothes was barely this side of going to the dentist. She also made me many clothes. The ones she bought and the ones she made were always the latest fashion and age-appropriate. My mom would never have me wearing "old lady" clothes!

I always took some sort of pride that I was so unlike her in this respect. My mother was so obsessed with her clothes, how could I possibly be anything like her? I loved jeans. Jeans and t-shirts in the summer, and jeans and sweatshirts in the winter were what I was most comfortable in.

But the truth was that I was as obsessed with my clothes as she was with hers. When I was four years old, the whole family was going out to dinner to a fancy restaurant. Everyone was all dressed up, and I came out with my favorite jeans on. After much screaming and yelling, my father finally said, "Let her wear the jeans and let's go!" In my thirties, I once told my co-workers that I would accept a dollar an hour less if I could only wear my jeans. Even now, I don't feel right or comfortable if I can't wear my jeans. We were both obsessed about clothes—just different clothes.

## The Greatest Gifts

If there was something my mom did which stood above all else, it was that she always supported me on all my misadventures. In my youth, I traveled from one state to another every one or two years. Different city, different job, and different state. Almost every time, she would travel cross country with me and stay until I had gotten settled. No matter how inappropriate she might think the move was, or how far away, she always supported me. She had always taught me to follow my heart, and she never faulted me for following her advice.

There were many lessons I learned from her in the two and a half years she spent in the nursing home. She helped me to understand so many aspects about our relationship and about myself. The most significant one was to stand up for myself by standing up to her. She had always taught me to "look out for number one, because no one else will." Toward the end, it turned out I had to make a choice between her and me. I chose me. That's exactly the way she would have wanted it.

\* \* \* \* \*

Point to Remember:

The gifts that I write about here are *my* gifts, *personal* gifts. They probably don't apply to you. Discover *your* gifts and you will be richer for it.

*Excerpt from My Journal:*
Another indication of her indomitable spirit: several days ago she complained because she kept dropping her silverware. She said she needed something to strengthen her hands. I mentioned a squeezing thing that I had seen in her drawer. She immediately started using it and told me today that she hasn't dropped a fork since she started using it. She never gives up. What a tremendous lesson—never give up.

## Chapter 11
## Endgame: Death and Dying

### To the Cornfield

Occasionally, while taking care of aging and infirm parents, when you feel tired, cranky, and overwhelmed with the mental and physical energy required, sometimes a stray thought crosses your mind, "I wish they were dead." Then the gravity of the thought strikes you, and you quickly brush it aside as if it wasn't borne of your own thoughts. It's a terrible thought. It's a guilt producing thought. But the thought in and of itself is not bad.

I left the house one day for a short walk and accidentally left the front door wide open. About halfway to my destination I realized it and worried that our old indoor cat might accidentally escape outside. At that time, she was way past her prime and a little on the senile side, meowing most of the night and keeping us awake. Although I loved the cat, I thought maybe it wouldn't be so bad if she got out and didn't make it back home.

When the original *Twilight Zone* was on television, with Rod Serling as the host, there was one episode about a little boy with supernatural powers. Whenever someone angered him in any way, he sent that person off to the cornfield, never to return.

When the cat event happened, I realized how easy it would be to get a "cornfield" mentality. The cat is keeping you up at night, send her to the cornfield. Taking care of your aging mother consumes more time than you expected, send her to the cornfield. Your husband starts annoying you, send him to the cornfield. After a while, you'd be all alone!

I've read about and heard about people who after their parent dies, they talk about "getting their life back." I honestly don't think this is an insult to the parent. I think part of "getting life back" would be a life where the parent is whole and "parental" again. That comment, I think, is a longing for the way life used to be.

*Some thoughts that you may have during these troubling times may make you feel guilty. Forgive yourself. Thoughts cannot hurt anyone. Don't feel guilty for a part of you that longs for the way things were.*

### Compassion or Conscience?

About a year after my mother entered the nursing home, I wrote a sad letter filled with angst to a friend. In the letter, I mentioned some of the chores that I did for my mother, such as handling her insurance and finances, and running errands for her. I asked my friend if I was a bad daughter because I didn't want to do some of the things that I did for her. Then I asked if I was a good daughter for doing them anyway.

Was I either one, good or bad? After some time to reflect, I decided that I was just a daughter, no more, no less. Even when there are other brothers and sisters, there is often one person in a family who takes on the responsibility for the aging parent. Why does that person do it? Do they love the parent more than their other siblings? Or is it a more defined sense of guilt?

I couldn't imagine dumping my mother somewhere and forgetting about her. How guilty and uncaring that would have made me feel! But my going to see her all the time, doing things for her, bringing her things that I knew she liked—while all of those things may have made her feel good, they also made me feel good on some level. Did I do them for her, or did I do them for me? Were my motives borne of compassion or borne of guilt? Does it matter? Every time I spoke to or saw my mother, I always closed with, "I love you." I made her feel good, I met all her needs, I made sure she was well taken care of, and I made her happy. Does it matter what my motives were? Do I even know what my motives were?

> *If your parent is happy and well taken care of because of actions that you have taken, it doesn't matter what initiated those actions. If the end is happiness, the means don't matter.*

## Grief or Relief

One beautiful, sunny day when I went to visit my mother, it was a sunny day inside, too. Usually, clouds of guilt, control, or unhappiness hung over our visits. This day, though, felt happy. At one point my mother said to me, "I'm sorry that it's difficult for me to show my feelings. It's just not something that I can do." I told her that I appreciated her saying that; and that even those simple words made me feel better. Then we had a long conversation starting with how she was brought up, and ending with how different she and I were. It was a warm and wonderful conversation that left us both feeling loved. I left that day with a smile instead of the hurt and veiled pain that usually accompanied me.

A part of me longed for her to die after that pleasant visit. So few of our visits left me feeling loved and loving that I wanted to preserve that feeling. So often I left there feeling defeated, and I didn't want that to be the last feeling I had toward my mother before she died. It would have made it so pleasant if I could remember for eternity how loving she was that day. Now, I don't know how it will turn out to be. She insults or taunts me often. Even though I always say, "I love you," at the end of each conversation and each visit, that's not always how I feel. How will I feel if she dies after doing something that makes me feel bad?

A friend of mine called this morning to say that her mother had died. She told me the story through tears, of her mother's hospitalization, her surgery, her near recovery, and then her death. She sobbingly told me of how much she missed her mom. Her grief touched me. I wanted to hug her. I wanted to hold her in my arms, comfort her, and feel her grief.

A part of me felt that feeling her grief would be as close as I would ever get to my own. After all the insults and guilt trips through the years, and especially the intensity of them the past two years, I didn't think that when my mother died I would have any grief left. My mother had already wiped it all away with her harsh words. I was afraid that at the end, all I would feel, could feel, was relief.

*This was written before my mother died. I was only guessing at not being able to feel the grief. But again, there is no way to know what you might feel when suddenly your parent is no longer in your life.*

## Advance Directives

Advance directives come in many forms, and rules regarding them vary from state to state. These documents state whether you want life support, resuscitation, and what type of medical treatment you would or would not want.

Often your parent will have already signed a document like this. Or, perhaps they have signed a document known as Durable Power of Attorney, which gives the designated person the ability to decide for the parent.

My mother had already signed both types of documents. Her wishes were not to be resuscitated, and she depended on me to make sure those wishes were followed. Even so, it was a weighty issue on my mind. I felt that by pointing out the document, I was condemning my mother to a death sentence. Which, in reality, is what the document was designed for. My mother had no desire to be on life support to extend a life not worth living. She was ninety-four years old, and she knew if it came to that, it was time to go. Still, I felt some anxiety over the situation.

One would think that after a document like this is signed, you never have to deal with it again. That is not always the case. With hospitals and doctors afraid of litigation, or even just double checking to be sure since it is literally a life or death decision, you are often called on to make the decision again—or in more detail.

Many times during my mother's final months, I was asked about the exact parameters of the initial request. One time a doctor asked me if her heart started beating erratically, should he give her chemicals to fix it. I said yes. Then he asked if her heart stopped beating, should he use the defibrillator. I said no. That was exactly what she did not want. But having to answer those questions—almost to have to make the decision repeatedly—is a taxing circumstance during an already emotional time.

*Make sure your parent's advance directive is as clear as possible. If you are asked questions later, be strong. You are doing what your parent wanted you to do.*

## Ghosts and Other Hauntings

A good friend of mine told me to be sure that I was with my mother when she died. At the time, I felt that moment might be imminent. No one would have guessed that she would be going strong more than two years later. But those words continued to haunt me during almost her entire stay at the nursing home. On the many times she went to the emergency room for heart or stroke problems, I panicked if I didn't think I would be there "in time."

When you look at it logically, it is a fool's errand. Unless you are with your parent twenty-four hours a day, there is no way you can be certain you will be present at the time of passing. Even if your parent is living with you and you spend virtually all your time together, who is to say they won't pass on while you are preparing a meal or using the restroom? There is no way to predict when a parent will die, and no way to "arrange" for your presence there.

Sometimes there will be an illness that is clearly getting worse every day, and you can visibly see the end coming. But, in cases where death is from a heart attack, stroke, or even just "old age," it is chance that determines if you're there or not.

Allowing myself to be haunted by that advice was unrealistic. During one of my mother's emergency room visits, I mentioned my friend's advice to her doctor. His response was that all the past moments that we had spent together before were more important than the single moment of death.

A nurse told me a sad story of an old man whose family gathered around his bed as he lay dying. They were so involved in conversations about their own lives, they didn't even notice when he had passed. Sometimes you can die alone even with a roomful of people.

Although no one likes the thought of your parent dying alone, and the thought of it evokes strong feelings of guilt, most times it is out of your control. My mother mentioned dying in her sleep as a friend of hers had. She thought that would be a peaceful way to pass on. Dying in the middle of a pleasant dream is a suitable ending after a long life well spent.

> You may be there when your parent dies, or you may not. Most times, it is out of your control. Don't become preoccupied with something that is out of

your hands. All your previous moments together were more important than this one.

## Put a Smile on the Grim Reaper

Let me say upfront that I do not advocate lying. I am not a liar, I do not believe in lying, and I think unequivocally that it is the wrong thing to do. But, there are always exceptions. If your parent is dying, is in pain, and is afraid of dying, even if you do not believe in a benevolent, loving God, I suggest you tell your parent that is who is waiting. What does it gain anyone to say that you think your parents are going to hell? There is no downside to telling them about love. I don't think a lie will be counted against you if it helps someone to pass in a gentle and peaceful manner. If your parent is afraid of dying, and it is obvious their death is imminent, comfort them in whatever way you can. Even if you have to lie. Keep in mind, however, that your beliefs of heaven or hell, a benevolent or a fearsome God, are only beliefs. You could be wrong. It might not be a lie, after all.

My mother had a roommate who spent several months in the fetal position. The nurses propped her into a wheelchair for meals and to use the restroom, but she spent most of her daytime hours in the fetal position. She had few visitors and seemed to get little joy from their visits. I kept asking myself why was she even alive? I think the answer was that she was afraid to die. If someone had talked to her about a loving God and a loving passing, perhaps she would not have struggled so long to hold on to such a meager existence.

During my mother's nursing home days, another gentleman was way past "ready to die." This gentleman had lived a wild and raucous life, and had done all the wrong things. He feared meeting his maker and being held accountable for all his wrong doings. His traditional religious upbringing, instead of comforting him in his time of need, caused him much suffering and needless worry. He was in pain, his time had come—and yet he was grasping at life because of his fears of what awaited him on the other side of death.

During one of many times my mother had been hospitalized for congestive heart failure, it seemed like this was it and she was going to die. I stood in the emergency room as her chest heaved up and down painfully. I watched her blood pressure rise unbelievably high and then drop dramatically. She could barely talk and breathing was painful. I thought, once again, that this was "it." Holding her hand, I told her to let go gently, not to hang on for my benefit, to relax and let go. My mother, tough as a tri-athlete, came through that episode fine, as well as many more like it. She never mentioned the words that I had spoken to her—I'm not sure if it was because she was too out of it to hear them—or if she only chose not to mention it. When I told the social worker what had happened, she said that it was good to give her "permission to die." She said many people want to hold on to their parents so bad, they don't give them the freedom to pass when it's their time to go.

*Give your parent a peaceful end time, even if you have to say something that you feel is against your personal beliefs. Instill in your parent that the next life is a beautiful and loving place. Peace and love are the only things that matter at times like this. Give your parent permission to die. Don't hold onto them for your own peace of mind and comfort. Now is the time to be selfless and give them the freedom to leave in peace.*

## Preparing for a Parent's Death

I'll start by saying that you can't. When I was much younger, I decided to learn how to hang glide. I went to a mini-course on it and then could try it for myself. They buckled me into the required harness, and attached me to a big bulky-winged hang glider. Right on the edge of a tall hill, I stood there bent over and scared to death. They said, "Are you ready?" Although I said yes because I felt I had to, the voice in my head screamed, "No, no!" How could I possibly be ready? I had never done that before. I had the knowledge, but the experience was something there was no way to imagine.

That's how I look at "preparing for a parent's death." You may think you're ready. You may have the knowledge you need and the emotional foundation that you think will get you through the process. Your parent may have been on the verge of death for years. But if you've never been through the experience before, there is no way you can know how you will react.

Since your birth, your parent has always been in your life. Whether they played an active role or not, a supportive or a hurtful role, it all adds up to the unknown emotional angst of the situation. Even if your parent is in a long-term coma or has severe dementia, it doesn't matter. They are still in your life, in their limited way. I always felt that my mom died when she had her stroke, although she lived with most of her cognition for more than two years beyond that. None of that matters.

They are still in your life. They are still the symbol of what they once were. You can't foresee your reaction to something that has never occurred before. Like me perched up on that tall hill—you may think you're ready, but in your heart you know that's not true. Nothing in your life has prepared you to lose a parent.

> *Don't fool yourself into thinking that you're "ready" or "prepared" for your parent's death. Nothing in your life has prepared you for this unimaginable event. No one knows the range of emotions and reactions to grief that we might go through at that time. Prepare not to be prepared.*

## The Rest of the Story

My husband and I had just returned from Utah to spend Easter with his family and especially to see his mother who was dying of cancer. We had spent twenty hours in airports and airplanes and felt exhausted. I had picked up a bad cold on our final overnight flight. It was the kind where you can't breathe at all and your nose just keeps running.

We walked into the house and found two messages on our answering machine. Both messages were from the same day. One was from Cathy, a nurse from the nursing home, saying that Mom wasn't feeling good, and they decided to send her to the emergency room.

Immediately, I felt bad because I had forgotten to tell the nursing home where I'd be during the long weekend. I also didn't know when the messages had arrived.

The second message was from a doctor at the hospital who wanted to talk about admitting my mother into the hospital. I called the doctor (not her regular doctor, because he was out of town on vacation) but couldn't reach him.

I called the nursing home, and Cathy said that Mom hadn't felt good and asked to go to the doctor. Cathy felt that she should go. When I reached the doctor, he said that Mom came in for congestive heart and breathing problems, but that was not why he wanted to admit her. He said the levels of some of her medication were excessively high and he wanted to monitor them. Also, a couple readings on her kidneys were off. I asked if I needed to come in, and he said no, that it was routine.

I tried calling Mom's room, but couldn't get through. My husband and I went to sleep. Early the next morning I called Mom's room, and the doctor answered the phone. He said that she had deteriorated overnight and that her kidney readings had gone down. He said it didn't look good.

I went in immediately. She lay there, sleeping, struggling for breath with her chest going up and down hard. The nurse woke her and told her that her daughter was there. She turned toward me and looked at me, but I'm not sure if she focused. She couldn't squeeze my hand. But every once in a while, she would raise her eyebrows, seemingly to what I was saying. It didn't look good. I told her about the white light and about the people who loved her who would greet her. I told her that I would be fine, and that she should not worry about me. I told her to relax and let go. My cold was horrible and my mother was in intensive care with other critical patients.

So, I left. The next morning, a different doctor called to say that Mom had passed away fifteen minutes before.

Later, I thought about the moment the doctor called and told me she had died. When I thought about that moment, I felt relief. It wasn't the relief of not having to go through all that stuff anymore. It was the relief of her not having to endure that broken body and mind anymore. She is now free. She is now whole. I celebrate her wholeness.

> You never know when the end will come. The best you can do is make sure your parents are comfortable and comforted. And although they have left your world, remember they are now without pain and without infirmity in theirs.

Obituary

Writing an obituary is one of the last jobs you will do for your parent. The question is, when do you write it?

Some newspapers insist on writing the obituary themselves. If this is the case, make sure they come to you for the details rather than the funeral home. You will want to make sure they get the details right, and will want to see it before it gets printed. Write the obituary yourself, if possible. Someone close to the person would know what's important to include.

State what the person did for a living before they retired. Note any clubs they were in, hobbies they had, or volunteer work they did. Keep the list of surviving relatives short. It's better to save the space for something personal they would want to be remembered for.

Include the person's age, perhaps their birthday, and their date of death. Including the cause of death is optional. If the person lived in another state, you might want to send the obituary to a newspaper there, also.

*If possible, write the obituary yourself. If you can't do that, be sure to check it over before it's published. Include important information as well as something personal they might want to be remembered for.*

## The Vultures Descend

After my mother died, I thought my life would get simpler. Instead, it instantly became more complex. Two days after my mother's death, I spoke to my eldest brother on the phone. He said that he knew it was too soon, but as long as I was on the phone, he wanted to know how much money remained in my mother's account. I answered the question, but felt his timing was inappropriate.

A month later, while still paying the last of my mother's bills, and figuring out everything she stated in her will, I received an email from him. This one was short, rude, and to the point. He wanted to know exactly what was coming to him, and he wasn't polite in the asking.

My life was anything but quiet and calm at this time. Besides dealing with my mother's death and the subsequent work it involved, my husband needed surgery, and his mother had terminal cancer. It was not an easy time for me, and then I received my brother's email! His timing was terrible!

I was just angry enough to send back a snappy and aggressive email, which didn't help the situation at all. He wrote back an even worse email, which made me almost physically ill. With my husband's encouragement and guidance, I wrote an email that diffused the situation, but didn't concede to his outrageous demands. Finally, he was somewhat satisfied.

Just when I thought it was safe to turn on my computer, my youngest brother sent me an even worse email concerning my mother's funeral. At first, I was devastated at his accusations and complaints until I realized that my mother didn't have a funeral. She had a simple memorial service, and I had never claimed it was anything more than that. Following the lead of my previous successful email, I wrote an almost deferential letter back explaining the circumstances in detail. Again, it solved the problem. Another lesson learned: I didn't have to be aggressive and rude to get my point across.

The next vulture on the list was one that I hadn't expected—a creditor. It was a convoluted situation that I thought I had already handled. Wrong. Shortly after my mother's death, I received a letter that referred to my mother as the "decedent" (how did they even know she was gone?), and wanted to know how I planned to settle the debt. It was another blow that I wasn't prepared for at all.

> Vultures, known for circling the dead, can descend on you when you least expect it and when you're least prepared for it. Already in a vulnerable position because of your parent's death, they can come from all sides to get their

share of the spoils. Be strong and stand up to them as best as you can.

## And Then from Out of the Woodwork

A sibling, estranged from the family for forty years, came forth after receiving the attorney's letter. No matter that his last missive, sent after an ill-conceived invitation to his mother's ninetieth birthday party, was rude and threatening. Now, he wanted his fair share, even if he had to come three thousand miles to make sure he got it.

His first letter to the attorney bordered on rude, but civilized. In the letter, he indicated that he wanted to give me the benefit of the doubt. Although he thought I had "swindled" him in some manner, he didn't want to do any name calling until he had all the facts.

But, even after he got all the facts in the form of a previous will from more than ten years earlier, he still couldn't be convinced that I wasn't cheating him. Nothing I said or did could convince him otherwise.

> Sometimes, when family members don't get what they thought they would get or what they wanted, they may blame you for the outcome. No matter how pure your intentions or how innocent you are, it's still a difficult situation to handle.

## Grief—More than Just Tears

Grief feels different for everyone. For me, there were few tears, much introspection, much thinking of old memories—mostly good. I had already spent too much time thinking of the bad memories.

The fact that I had few tears bothered me. I knew I loved my mother. Despite the pain she caused me, I was aware that none of it had been done deliberately. What she ultimately "did" to me, was the result of all that had been "done" to her over a lifetime. She didn't want to hurt me. She only wanted to love me. It didn't always feel that way. So I tried to forgive her, and I loved her with all my heart. Parts of me also hated her. But the love was real, and the love was strong.

So why wasn't I crying? My mother died shortly before Mother's Day. The Friday before Mother's Day, I watched a Mother's Day special on television. It was for me, a half hour of flowing, cleansing tears. I felt cleaned out when the program finished. I also missed my mother tremendously.

But afterward, again, no tears. It bothered me because I thought I wasn't grieving. About that time I saw an article about grief in our local newspaper. It told of all the different symptoms of grief, including lack of energy, inability to concentrate, and low self-esteem. Now those I could identify with—especially low self-esteem! After my mother died, I felt out of place everywhere I went. I felt out of touch with any people that I was with. Mostly, I didn't feel like I fit in anywhere, which is a classic symptom of low self-esteem. So I was grieving after all! Just no tears!

Relief and understanding washed over me after I read that article. I not only had to contend with my mother's death, but I had to contend with my own guilt feelings because I thought I wasn't grieving. Finally, I understood that grief is more than tears.

Several months after her death, I realized what some of my anxiety stemmed from. I feared that other people would think I wasn't grieving or didn't love my mother because it didn't appear that I was grieving. I finally came to the realization that it doesn't matter what they think. What was important was that I knew how much I loved her, and I knew undoubtedly that she knew how much I loved her.

Even months after my mother's death, I felt a deep sense of loss whenever I read a recipe that she had given me or remembered a funny story that she had told me. Just when it feels like you are finished grieving, grief will sneak up on you and grab you by the heart.

> There are many symptoms of grief. If your grief doesn't include long bouts of crying, don't let it bother you. Everyone is different and everyone grieves in different ways. Grief is more than just tears.

\* \* \* \* \*

Points to Remember:

1. Some thoughts that you may have during these troubling times may make you feel guilty. Forgive yourself. Thoughts cannot hurt anyone. Don't feel guilty for a part of you that longs for the way things were.

2. If your parent is happy and well taken care of because of actions that you have taken, it doesn't matter what initiated those actions. If the end is happiness, the means don't matter.

3. There is no way to know what you might feel when suddenly your parent is no longer in your life.

4. Make sure your parent's advance directive is as clear as possible. If you are asked questions later, be strong. You are doing what your parent wanted you to do.

5. You may be there when your parent dies, or you may not. Most times, it is out of your control. Don't become preoccupied with something that is out of your hands. All your previous moments together were more important than this one.

6. Give your parent a peaceful end time, even if you have to say something that you feel is against your personal beliefs. Instill in your parent that the next life is a beautiful and loving place. Peace and love are the only things that matter at times like this. Give your parent permission to die. Don't hold onto them for your own peace of mind and comfort. Now is the time to be selfless and give them the freedom to leave in peace.

7. Don't fool yourself into thinking that you're "ready" or "prepared" for your parent's death. Nothing in your life has prepared you for this unimaginable event. No one knows the range of emotions and reactions to grief that we might go through at this time. Prepare not to be prepared.

8. You never know when the end will come. The best you can do is make sure your parents are comfortable and comforted. And although they have left your world, remember they are now without pain and without infirmity in theirs.

9. If possible, write the obituary yourself. If you can't do that, be sure to check it over before it's published. Include important information as

well as something personal they might want to be remembered for.

    10. Vultures, known for circling the dead, can descend on you when you least expect it and when you're least prepared for it. Already in a vulnerable position because of your parent's death, they can come from all sides to get their share of the spoils. Be strong and stand up to them as best as you can.

    11. Sometimes, when family members don't get what they thought they would get or what they wanted, they may blame you for the outcome. No matter how pure your intentions or how innocent you are, it's still a difficult situation to handle.

    12. There are many symptoms of grief. If your grief doesn't include long bouts of crying, don't let it bother you. Everyone is different and everyone grieves in different ways. Grief is more than just tears.

## *Excerpts from My Journal:*

I've noticed that some of my friends have kind of abandoned me. I guess it's only fair since that is what I do when faced by death. I don't know what to say, so I don't say anything. Now I realize that is so much worse. This is a time when I need more support, not to be abandoned.

When I told my cousin of her death, he commented that now we can answer our phone. He said what a horrible thing not to be able to answer your phone. Now I wait for her to call knowing she never will again.

Today we went to clean out her room at the nursing home. As I went through various stuff and considered keeping it, I could almost hear her voice in the background saying, "What do you need that junk for?"

Then, we ran into Mom's friend and next door neighbor. The woman, all teary-eyed, said how she couldn't believe it. She said that Mom had even walked to the ambulance in her walker. That's my mother—tough and determined right to the end.

www.ingramcontent.com/pod-product-compliance
Lightning Source LLC
Chambersburg PA
CBHW061639040426
42446CB00010B/1497